SCI FI

TV

From Twilight Zone
To Deep Space Nine

OTHER PIONEER BOOKS

•FISTS OF FURY: THE FILMS OF BRUCE LEE
Written by Edward Gross. March, 1990. $14.95, ISBN #1-55698-233-X
•WHO WAS THAT MASKED MAN? THE STORY OF THE LONE RANGER
Written by James Van Hise. March, 1990. $14.95, ISBN #1-55698-227-5
•PAUL MCCARTNEY: 20 YEARS ON HIS OWN
Written by Edward Gross. February, 1990. $9.95, ISBN #1-55698-263-1
•THE DARK SHADOWS TRIBUTE BOOK
Written by Edward Gross and James Van Hise. February, 1990. $14.95, ISBN#1-55698-234-8
•THE UNOFFICIAL TALE OF BEAUTY AND THE BEAST, 2nd Edition
Written by Edward Gross. $14.95, 164 pages, ISBN #1-55698-261-5
•TREK: THE LOST YEARS
Written by Edward Gross. $12.95, 128 pages, ISBN #1-55698-220-8
•THE TREK ENCYCLOPEDIA
Written by John Peel. $19.95, 368 pages, ISBN#1-55698-205-4
•HOW TO DRAW ART FOR COMIC BOOKS
Written by James Van Hise. $14.95, 160 pages, ISBN#1-55698-254-2
•THE TREK CREW BOOK
Written by James Van Hise. $9.95, 112 pages, ISBN#1-55698-256-9
•BATMANIA
Written by James Van Hise. $14.95, 176 pages, ISBN#1-55698-252-6

Designed and Edited by Hal Schuster
with the assistance of David Lessnick

Library of Congress Cataloging-in-Publication Data
James Van Hise, 1949—
          Sci Fi TV From Twilight Zone to Deepspace Nine

          1.   Sci Fi TV From Twilight Zone to Deepspace Nine (television)
     I. Title

First Printing, 1993

<u>Dedicated to all that has come before. . . .</u>

JAMES VAN HISE writes about film, television and comic book history. He has written numerous books on these subjects, including BAT-MANIA, TREK: THE NEXT GENERATION, THE TREK CREW BOOK, STEPHEN KING & CLIVE BARKER: THE ILLUSTRATED GUIDE TO THE MASTERS OF THE MACABRE and HOW TO DRAW ART FOR COMIC BOOKS: LESSONS FROM THE MASTERS. He is the publisher of MIDNIGHT GRAFFITI, in which he has run previously unpublished stories by Stephen King and Harlan Ellison. Van Hise resides in San Diego along with his wife, horses and various other animals.

My Sincere
Good Wishes,
Martin Landau

1992 marked a long-predicted inroad into the cable television market__the debut of the SCI-FI CHANNEL. With other special channels already existing in this ever-growing extension of the medium, from the shopping channels, to the Family Channel to the Nashville Network to American Movie Classics to the Playboy Channel and the Comedy Channel, it was inevitable that another large potential audience would be served.

The success of STAR WARS, E.T. and STAR TREK proved that science fiction was not just a non-repeatable phenomenon as some Hollywood wags attempted to call it. Science fiction has been staking out a corner of television since the Fifties and has grown as the world around it changes and grows. Science fiction is a product of the times in which we live. In the Fifties it seems a distant realm of storytelling, but in the Sixties we landed on the moon—a feat that few in 1959 would have ever believed could come to pass in the span of a single decade.

Kurt Vonnegut once had to defend why his early work occupied so much of itself with science fiction concepts, but he explained (often) that science fiction was the only literature which even considered the future, or even that there would be one. Too often contemporary literature seemed to act as though things would always be as they are now. While in the beginning, television science fiction was not all that adventurous in the concepts it explored, pioneers like Rod Serling realized that anything which required a leap of imagination would be adventurous to a large segment of the population. This is why even thought THE TWILIGHT ZONE may often seem quaint by today's standards, thirty years ago it was like nothing many had ever seen before. The science fiction film was still very much in its infancy in those days. Even in theaters, such fare formed only a small percentage of the total Hollywood output.

Luckily, television was an omnivorous creature, with several channels and twenty-four hours a day to fill. It was inevitable that science fiction would get its turn at bat. This rotation took many forms, from the simplistic approach of Irwin Allen to the more challenging reach of Gene Roddenberry and his team of creative dreamers. Thanks to the imagination of an actor named Patrick McGoohan over in England, American audiences were able to see that science fiction could even infect the familiar world, twisting it with satire and social comment which wasn't as far removed from our own reality as we might have thought.

The Seventies seemed to hit a fallow period at first. STAR TREK was still considered a failure as the decade opened, and any chance of reviving it seemed the most

INTRODUCTION
SCI FI TV

hopeless of pipe dreams. The rather ordinary UFO and the less than well crafted SPACE: 1999 did not bode well as these shows did not aim as high as the subjects they explored. But STAR TREK, a seemingly deceased enterprise, kept nibbling at the corners of our collective conscience and in syndication the failed science fiction series became the springboard for a motion picture revival and finally two new television series.

Science fiction was off and running again and the Nineties seem to be ushering in a new cycle of SF on TV. Not only is DEEP SPACE NINE beginning what will undoubtedly be a long and successful run in syndication, but even the networks are testing the imaginative waters again with such shows as SPACE RANGERS and TIME-TRAX. A new network, being started by Warner Brothers, is testing a two-hour pilot named BABYLON 5 which promises to go beyond even the highest expectations of STAR TREK fans.

It was once thought that science fiction was a genre whose television audience was small. Think again!

**—James Van Hise,
January 1993**

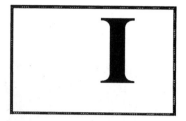

While we generally regard the age of science fiction television to have begun with THE TWILIGHT ZONE in 1959, more primitive efforts existed before that. The earliest one was CAPTAIN VIDEO AND HIS VIDEO RANGERS which ran in various lengths, and mostly in rerun, from 1949 until 1955. Richard Coogan played the title character in its first year but Al Hodge is the best-known Captain Video, playing the role from 1951-1955. The show was popular enough to offer premiums and other toy tie-ins but it's virtually unknown among modern fans of TV shows.

Even BUCK ROGERS had an early TV show; a half-hour program from April 1950 to January 1951. In its brief life two different actors, Kem Dibbs and Robert Pastene played the title character. Like most early TV shows, these were performed live and recorded on kinescopes. But even when a new version was done in 1979, the writing hadn't improved much.

The best remembered of the Fifties sci-fi adventures shows remains TOM CORBETT, SPACE CADETT. Tom Corbett was played by Frankie Thomas and even though the series only ran from Oct. 1950 to Sept. 1952, it eventually played on all three networks in succession during that period, and was often seen three nights a week. The special effects budget, even though primitive by today's standards, outclassed the even cheaper CAPTAIN VIDEO, which the show was produced to cash in on the popularity of. So even in the earliest days of the then-new medium, science fiction was an important genre to be considered by the producers.

As popular as TOM CORBETT was SPACE PATROL, starring Ed Kemmer as Commander Buzz Corey. It ran on ABC from June 1951 to June 1952 but continued as a locally produced west coast series until 1955. It was a half-hour show on network but expanded to one-hour when it became locally produced by a Los Angeles station. Remember that in the Fifties New York was initially the main production center for network television, a fact which didn't change until the late Fifties when Hollywood took over much of the production business for television.

IN THE BEGINNING

The first science fiction anthology show was the short-lived OUT THERE which ran from October 1951 to January 1952 on CBS. Also shot live, it incorporated filmed special effects sequences. While TOM CORBETT and the other sci-fi series then were clearly children's' adventure shows, OUT THERE tried to be a step up and

adapted stories from the science fiction pulp magazines of the day, but it just didn't catch on during its brief incarnation.

TALES OF TOMORROW had much better luck on ABC and ran for 84 episodes from August 1951 to June 1953. Due to the volume of episodes made, this show is better remembered and more shows are circulating today among collectors. James Dean had an early role in one episode and the show even featured adaptations of such stories as "The Crystal Egg" by H.G. Wells and Jules Verne's 20,000 LEAGUES UNDER THE SEA, albeit condensed quite a bit in the case of the latter.

While the Buster Crabbe Flash Gordon serials proved popular when run on television first in 1951, the attempt to capture this audience with a new FLASH GORDON series in 1953 wasn't as successful. Although 38 episodes were made of this syndicated show starring Steve Holland, it wasn't that well received.

A much better job was done on CAPTAIN MIDNIGHT, starring Richard Webb. Shot on film with top special effects for its day, this 1953-55 series was later syndicated under the name JET JACKSON, with every mention of the character's name redubbed to avoid having to pay the copyright holder of the Captain Midnight name. It's production level was on par with that of SUPERMAN which still plays today to appreciative audiences, although the Fifties setting of the stories cannot be mistaken.

THE MAN OF STEEL

SUPERMAN was, of course, the premiere science fiction series of the Fifties, running from 1952 to 1957. Out of 104 episodes produced, about the last third were actually made in color, which no one had the capability of seeing on their TV's in those days. When 13 those episodes were actually syndicated in color in the late Sixties, it was a big deal to those of us who had just gotten color TV's in our homes. This series was made to capitalize on the huge success of the two Columbia motion picture serials starring Superman which were made in 1948 and 1950.

Kirk Alyn, who had played Superman in the serials, was offered the TV role but turned it down as he was determined to break the typecasting the serial had caused him, and even though he worked in films in the Fifties, he never really shook that image. When George Reeves went on strike for higher pay, Kirk Alyn was approached again and he turned it down, telling them that Reeves deserved whatever he wanted because of how relentless the typecasting would be for him.

This had already been proven when a small role Reeves had in the motion picture FROM HERE TO ETERNITY was cut due to the reaction of preview audiences to seeing Reeves on the screen. When George Reeves died in 1957 (and some still question whether it was suicide) he was planning to film a new season of SUPERMAN, including an opportunity to direct some episodes. Although dated, this series remains quite popular with fans of all ages. Strangely enough, the show has a timeless quality about it as it seems to recall not so much the Fifties as it does a period which *seems* like the Fifties but is outside of it altogether.

The one Fifties outer space series which managed to survive in syndication in the Sixties was ROCKY JONES, SPACE RANGER. Produced from January 1954-1955, the series was shot on film with pretty decent special effects, particularly for the lead's spaceship, the Orbit Jet. "Jet" was the buzzword of the Fifties as it conjured up images of modern technology. The show starred Richard Crane (who appeared in some adventure serials in the Fifties) as the title character.

He had a kid sidekick as well as a female assistant. Unlike most female aides, this one wasn't as much a shrinking violet as Flash Gordon's Dale Arden was. In fact women often had prominent roles in various storylines, often as an empress or some such. Only thirty-nine episodes were made but in memory it seemed like more. Various TV actors appeared in the series, including John Banner (Sgt. Schultz on HOGAN'S HEROES) as a villain in one storyline.

WONDERFUL WORLD OF SYNDICATION

Another series which played a great deal in syndication was SCIENCE FICTION THEATER (with your host Truman Bradley). Seventy-eight episodes were produced from 1955-1957. The anthology series dealt with such subjects as UFO's and even one about a baby woolly mammoth which was thawed and brought back to life. The series was much closer to what was being explored in some science fiction magazines of the day (albeit these were idea stories, not space opera or adventure stories). One episode even dealt with the strange effects of a drug called LSD. In the Fifties.

MEN INTO SPACE, which ran for only one year, was a near future science fiction series. Starring William Lundigan as Col. Edward McCauley, he was America's premiere Astronaut. The series dealt with what space exploration might be like in the late twentieth century. The series ran hot and cold on how Russians were treated (depending on if we were being friendly to the USSR from one week to the next). One of the last episodes took Co. McCauley to Mars where he orbited the planet, but when the show was canceled we never got to see the series explore Mars the way it had explored the surface of the Moon.

The Sixties took many wild directions in the realm of science fiction television. That this wasn't the Fifties any more was demonstrated with MY FAVORITE MARTIAN which ran for three years, from 1963-66 and it's still some of the best remembered work of either Bill Bixby or Ray Walston. The premise of the show was pretty thin. A Martian (Walston) crashes on Earth and befriends Tim O'Hara (Bill Bixby). Through typical sitcom back-against-the-wall situations, Tim calls Walston "Uncle Martin" and that becomes his name for the duration.

Periodically Martin would try to get his mini-spaceship fixed and return to Mars but it never happened. Uncle Martin had antenna which he would raise whenever he wanted to become invisible, a gag used recently on the Halloween episode of PICKET FENCES, a

13

series where Walston has a recurring supporting role.

THE KING

Irwin Allen was the king of science fiction television on the Sixties. VOYAGE TO THE BOTTOM OF THE SEA ran for four years (1964-68) and lasted 110 episodes, although it is rarely seen in syndication today. VOYAGE was a near future science fiction series, but it used its centerpiece, a glitzy-looking submarine called The Seaview, around which they spun stories of giant undersea monsters, invaders from space and various other men in monster suit stories.

Every character on the show took every story dead seriously, no matter how absurd the proceedings. Even before STAR TREK, the Seaview was hurling sparks this way and that whenever control panels shorted out, in spite of the fact that even in 1964 there was something called a circuit-breaker which would prevent light shows like that from happening. Buy hey, this is television!

LOST IN SPACE soon followed, in 1965, but what began as a series approach to the concept, transmogrified in just a handful of episodes into the live-action cartoon which its fans came to love. In 1966, Irwin Allen launched THE TIME TUNNEL, the least successful of his Sixties series. Starring James Darren and Robert Colbert as two reluctant time-travelers, for one year they explored the most obvious moments in history you could think of.

When they started running out of ideas, instead of doing a little research and finding the really

interesting moments in time to explore, they started fighting aliens with silver faces. The series had already exhausted itself by the time it was mercifully canceled. This is not to say that more couldn't have been done, but Irwin Allen was just not an adventurous enough producer to consider doing it.

Less shrill and explosive was THE INVADERS. Although it only ran a year and a half (from January 1967 to September 1968), this Quinn-Martin series tackled a more realistic take on the invaders from space drama. Set in the present day, the stories were both mysteries and thrillers, done more in the tone of THE FUGITIVE and light years away from the Irwin Allen style of grandiose adventure. Still, by the time the show began to wind down, viewers began to wish that the show would cut loose a bit more and not be quite so reserved and restrained. While the show attempted to explore its subject within intelligent limits, a little more OUTER LIMITS style weirdness and wildness would have served it better in the long run.

SILLINESS SELLS

That science fiction was running its course toward the end of the Sixties was ably demonstrated with LAND OF THE GIANTS, an anemic and silly Irwin Allen series which nonetheless outlasted TIME TUNNEL by a year. This was no less astonishing for the fact that each episode told virtually the same story.

People from our Earth in the near future, enter a parallel universe Earth populated by giants (by our standards, and it must be a parallel Earth as they all speak

English). The "little people" try to get their aircraft, the Spindrift, repaired and are constantly captured by giants and then must escape. Periodically someone else from Earth would turn up in a story, and once a giant was shrunk down to human size to infiltrate our merry band. It was only fitting then that in another episode one of the humans was enlarged to giant size to infiltrate them. It was pretty tedious stuff, but then so was F TROOP and that's being remade as a theatrical motion picture. Go figure.

Gerry and Sylvia Anderson, who had success in the Sixties with the science fiction Supermarionation shows SUPERCAR, THUNDERBIRDS, JOE 90, CAPTAIN SCARLET and FIREBALL XL5, were finally given the chance to produce life action shows in the Seventies.

The 1970 series UFO starred Ed Bishop as Commander Straker and was set in the dizzying future time of 1980 when we had an elaborate manned moonbase and futuristic vessels which could easily fly from the Earth to the Moon and back again. Filmed in England the series was also set in England. Although it tried very hard, the series had that restrained quality of too many British shows and never tried to kick loose and fly the way the more wild and way out American produced shows did. Considering that the producers were counting on the United States market for its profitability, this proved to be a draw-

back and only 26 episodes were produced. It is little seen today.

AMERICAN FAILURE AND A BRITISH HIT

This was soon followed by SPACE 1999 which did last for two years and tried valiantly to be an ersatz American show (even hiring American TV stars to try and trick us). After two years the producers were still trying to figure out where they went wrong and not succeeding in mending the show's glaring flaws.

DR. WHO is a peculiar British show which existed in one

The earliest science fiction television show was CAPTAIN VIDEO AND HIS VIDEO RANGERS which ran in various lengths, and mostly in rerun, from 1949 until 1955. Richard Coogan played the title character in its first year but Al Hodge is the best-known Captain Video.

form or another for over twenty years. Periodically going in and out of production, the series has remained a perennial favorite in England. In the US the Tom Baker episodes are those most commonly seen. He is most Americanfans' favorite Dr. Who. The reason there is more than one version is that whenever an actor left the series, Dr. Who would undergo a metamorphosis and change his appearance.

In this way the title character was always the same person, even though his appearance would change periodically. Most episodes were shot on videotape and by American standards this makes them look cheap and low budget, only because they were cheap and low budget. Further complicating this is the fact that British shows used to do exterior footage on film so that scenes on the show would switch back and forth between film and video with glaring regularity, an aspect which tended to annoy American audiences. Episodes are each a half-hour long (usually) and are serials, running from a handful of episodes to stories which were much longer. The series has a legion of fans and hundreds of books based on the series have been produced in England.

THE IMMORTAL was another low-key approach to science fiction. The show ran for one year as Christopher George, a man who discovers that he is immortal, flees from the bad guys who want to capture him and sell his blood to the highest bidder. It was just THE FUGITIVE given a different reason to run and didn't even scratch the surface of the possibilities inherent in such an idea. Typical mundane television in which the science fiction element is both played up, to make it seem different, while also being played down in order to make everything that happens seem safe, comfortable and familiar.

MOVING INTO THE 70'S

THE STARLOST was produced in 1973 by a Canadian company and dealt with a generation ship in deep space where the occupants have been there so long that they are descendants of those who first boarded the ship. The occupants also no longer know they're on a spacecraft. Created by Harlan Ellison, the series was so poorly produced that Ellison removed his

name and put his pseudonym Cordwainer Bird (as in "for the birds") on the show. Ellison's friend Walter Koenig made a couple appearances in an attempt to liven things up, but the shot on videotape production just never flew.

PLANET OF THE APES was a short-lived television series spun off the successful series of five motion pictures. But in translating the concept to television, nearly everything which made the films popular was changed, and without explanation. Humans couldn't talk in the movies but did all the time in the series, making the two astronauts from the 20th century no different from any other human in the ape-dominated world of the future.

This may well have been done because having apes being given 90% of the dialogue would have made it tough to find actors who'd be willing to appear on the show and do mime every week. The series was one of those crash and burn stories where high hopes were held but they just didn't pay off. The one hour series has been recut into a group of two-hour TV movies which turn up in syndication periodically.

THE SIX MILLION DOLLAR MAN starred Lee Majors as a cyborg. One arm and both legs were replaced with bionic parts after his plane crashes, and he becomes a modern day version of Superman. Whenever he went into action he was shown moving in slow-motion, a gimmick which got annoying quickly. The show lasted for four years nonetheless and produced a spin-off, THE BIONIC WOMAN starring Lindsay Wagner which lasted for two and one-half years.

When the 1976 movie LOGAN'S RUN proved to be popular, it was spun off into a TV series which only lasted for four months. It was another version of THE FUGITIVE which employed its far future science fiction setting as little as possible, and thereby explored its concept not all. Episodes were done which were little more than remakes of the classic story "The Most Dangerous Game" as well as of the STAR TREK episode "Charlie X" without doing anything more than the obvious with the elements at hand. Shows such as this have made non-SF fans who tuned in think that all science fiction is dull and boring.

NOT SO HOT SCI-FI

As though to prove the truth of this single-handedly, Glenn Larson created BATTLESTAR GALACTICA and its laughable follow-up GALACTICA 1980. Dull copies of elements done successfully in STAR WARS, these two series were populated with characters who were almost always dullards slogging their way through hopeless scripts.

Even worse was Larson's two-season wonder BUCK ROGERS, which ran from September 1979 to April 1981. Starring Gil Gerard as the twentieth century man who awakens in the world of 500 years from now after being shot into space and returning to Earth, the series was silly and populated with "cute" robots and derivative special effects. An attempt to revamp it was made for the second season by introducing Hawk, a bird-man alien played by

Thom Christopher, but the scripts just never took advantage of what they had at hand.

Little of note appeared in the rest of the Eighties, except for THE RAY BRADBURY THEATRE. Written by Bradbury himself, this half-hour series adapts Bradbury's classic stories for the TV screen, often with marvelous (if low budget) results. The series began on Showtime and now appears, with new episodes, on the USA cable network.

The gem in the crown of anthology television remains THE TWI-LIGHT ZONE. All anthology shows produced since then have been measured against this series, and inevitably come up short.

THE TWILIGHT ZONE was, first and foremost, a writer's show. Three writers provided the bulk of the scripts for the series: Charles Beaumont, Richard Matheson, and Rod Serling.

Rod Serling was not just a writer for THE TWILIGHT ZONE— he was the show's creator, and the face and voice most associated with the series. Rod Serling was born on Christmas Day, 1924, in Syracuse, New York. He grew up in another New York town, Binghampton, with his parents and his younger brother Bob.

Rod Serling joined the Army right out of high school in 1945. Despite his late entry into World War II, he saw action in the Philippines as a paratrooper and was wounded. He found himself drawn towards writing while attending college on the G.I. Bill. In 1948, he married his wife Carol.

After winning a radio script contest, Serling turned pro. He had a short on-air career and started submitting script after script to radio dramas all over the country. Soon enough, he shifted his endeavors to a newer broadcast medium, television. One of his earliest sales, the 1953 drama "A Long Time Till dawn," starred James Dean before Dean made it big in films.

By 1955, the freelancing Serling had sold seventy-one television scripts of varying quality; his seventy-second, "Patterns," was performed on January 12 of that year as part of the Kraft Television Theater. This drama of a business power struggle, which starred Ed Begley, Everett Sloane, and Richard Kiley, catapulted Serling to critical and popular success, making his career overnight (after years of hard work on his part, as is usually the case). The show was even repeated a month later, which, in the television of those days, meant that it was performed live for a second time. Above all, it meant that Rod Serling would never be out of work again. In fact, he managed to sell many scripts that he had written years earlier in college.

A BIG SUCCESS

Financially successful, Serling received another critical boost in October 1956 when the second episode of a CBS series called PLAYHOUSE 90 was aired. "Requiem For A Heavyweight," starring Jack Palance, stands to this day as one of the classics of early television, and swept the television awards for that year.

Other PLAYHOUSE 90 successes followed: "The Comedian" and "The Dark Side of the Earth" in 1957 were followed by the next year's "The Rank and File" and

"A Town Has Turned To Dust." In 1959, his autobiographical drama, "The Velvet Alley" aired. That year also saw another landmark in Rod Serling's meteoric career: he began work on a half-hour science-fiction series called THE TWILIGHT ZONE.

Some people thought that this was a step down for such a highly-regarded writer. Interviewer Mike Wallace went so far as to ask Serling if he'd given up writing anything "serious" for television. The first TWILIGHT ZONE story, "The Time Element," was an hour-long expansion of a half-hour script Serling had written in college. It involves a man who travels back in time to Pearl Harbor on December 6, 1941, but cannot convince anyone of the imminent Japanese attack.

It was a struggle to get the story on the air, as the time traveler (played by William Bendix) dies at Pearl Harbor and is erased from all the years that followed. Even once the show was aired, host Arnaz felt obliged to come out and explain the story rationally, opening that the man's psychiatrist dreamt the entire story! But reviews and public response were strong, and Serling had another winner on his hands.

Serling still had to sell THE TWILIGHT ZONE with a pilot; "The Time Element" now belonged to the Desilu show. Bill Dozier, CBS' West Coast honcho (TV was still based in New York in these days) put Bill Self on the Zone scene. The first script, "The Happy Place," was too downbeat, so a second script, "Where Is Everybody?" was approved; this story of a man driven mad by an isolation experiment was filmed with Dan Duryea

in the key role, and THE TWILIGHT ZONE soon had a sponsor, General Foods. The pilot was aired and the series debuted on October 2, 1959. "Where Is Everybody" is actually a fairly weak story, but it was simple and easy for the network brass to understand. With the network complacent, Serling went on to write stories which were a bit more challenging than a man having a hallucination.

SCARY WRITERS

The series was a success. Week after week, viewers saw Jean Marsh as an android providing company for a lonely prisoner in space; David Wayne as a hypochondriac who makes a deal with the Devil; Gig Young as a man who returns to the scene— and time— of his childhood; and more. These and the rest of the first seven episodes were scripted by Serling; but the third, "The Last Flight," was written by another mainstay of THE TWILIGHT ZONE, Richard Matheson.

Richard B. Matheson (named after the 19th Century British explorer whose name had already been assumed as a stage name by the late Welsh actor now famous as Richard Burton) was born on February 20, 1926, in Allendale, New Jersey. After growing up in Brooklyn, Matheson, like Serling, served in the army during World War II. After majoring in journalism at the University of Missouri, Matheson embarked on a career in fiction, selling his first story, "Born of Man and Woman," to THE MAGAZINE OF FANTASY 7 SCIENCE FICTION. A prolific career in the genre ensued, and Matheson was drawn to California when Universal made the classic film adaptation of his novel THE SHRINKING MAN (with the adjective Incredible inserted; adjectives sold movies!) in 1956.

No less a writer than Stephen King cites Matheson as a major influence. Matheson's I AM LEGEND was made into a movie twice, cheaply but somewhat faithfully as THE LAST MAN ON EARTH starring Vincent Price, and later as the Charlton Heston vehicle THE OMEGA MAN. Matheson's own scripts include the Roger Corman Poe "adaptations" such as THE HOUSE OF USHER, THE RAVEN and THE PIT AND THE PENDULUM. In fact, not only does Matheson continue to write to the present day, but his son is also a respected writer.

Matheson's first TWILIGHT ZONE, "The Last Flight," involved a World War One pilot who abandons a companion to his fate at the hands of German pilots. The pilot winds up at a modern-day Air Force base, where he reassesses his actions and returns to his own time to sacrifice his life.

CLASSIC SCRIPTS

The next episode, "And When The Sky Was Opened," was scripted by Serling from a story by Matheson, and involved astronauts (including Jim Hutton) who return to Earth and vanish, even from the memories of others. "The Hitchhiker" was adapted by Serling from a radio play that was originally performed by Orson Welles on radio in the 1930s. In fact, Serling was on an adaptation roll: however, in some cases he improved on the original, notably in the case of "Time Enough At Last," which

marked the first of Burgess Meredith's appearances on THE TWILIGHT ZONE; this was the episode where he plays the bookish clerk saved from his tedious life by a nuclear war, only to break his glasses, rendering him unable to read.

The thirteenth episode, "Perchance To Dream," was an original tale by the highly original Charles Beaumont, the third of the great triad of TWILIGHT ZONE writers. A good friend of Richard Matheson, Beaumont had met Rod Serling a few years earlier, and had endeared himself to Serling by unabashedly saying that "The Velvet Alley" was the worst piece of writing he'd ever encountered.

On January 2, 1929, the man who would later adopt the pseudonym Charles Beaumont was born Charles LeRoy Nutt in Chicago. Stories of his strange family background are quite famous; among other things, his mother made him dress as a girl when he was a very young boy (later the source of his tale "Miss Gentillbelle"). Fortunately, the young Charles wound up being raised primarily by five aunts who, although themselves eccentric, did not suffer from his mother's problems in coping with reality.

A teenage science fiction fan, Charles Nutt dropped out of tenth grade to join the army— but was discharged after three months for back problems. After that it was one career after another: acting, science fiction illustration (as Charles McNutt), pianist, radio discjockey, dishwasher, animator (at MGM) and comic book editor, all the while writing stories that his agent, Forrest J. Ackerman, was unable to sell until AMAZING STORIES bought his tale "The Devil, You Say?" in 1950.

In 1954 he broke a top short story market, Hugh Hefner's Playboy, and was soon a regular contributor to that top-paying magazine. Television script work also joined his repertoire and he wrote for such diverse programs as ONE STEP BEYOND, SUSPENSE, WANTED, DEAD OR ALIVE, and HAVE GUN, WILL TRAVEL. (He also scripted the truly atrocious B-movie, QUEEN OF OUTER SPACE, which he always maintained was a parody that no one, except himself, realized was a joke.)

PERSONAL TWILIGHT ZONE

Beaumont died in February 1967 at the tender age of thirty-eight. He had been acting strange for a couple of years, and drinking heavily, but it turned out that his real problem was a degenerative disease of the brain similar to Alzheimer's. In the short years between the onset of his disease and his death, he often could not write. Another writer, Jerry Sohl, helped Beaumont meet his TWILIGHT ZONE contractual obligations by ghosting scripts for him.

Beaumont's first TWILIGHT ZONE script was "Perchance To Dream," based on his own short story of the same name. Here, a man tells his psychiatrist of a recurring dream in which he is being lured to his death by a gorgeous woman in a carnival funhouse; ultimately, he dies in the dream, leaving the shrink with a dead man on his office couch. Then Serling was back as scripter with a tale in which Ida Lupino played an aging movie actress along the lines of Nora Desmond who manages to somehow escape back into her old movies— literally.

The next episode, "The Four Of Us Are Dying," was scripted by Rod Serling from a short story by another writer whose name would be linked with THE TWILIGHT ZONE: George Clayton Johnson. Johnson was born on July 10, 1929 in Cheyenne, Wyoming. He grew up in a dysfunctional family—divorced parents, alcoholic mother, ect. . . After years of slipping behind in school, the fourteen year old Johnson was placed in a state orphanage, only to be returned to his mother a year later.

At 16, Johnson was on his own and a year later joined the army. He learned drafting, which enabled him to support his new family in California after his discharge. Writing soon became his calling. In the second season of THE TWILIGHT ZONE, he wrote an original script for the series that launched his career in earnest.

AN ADAPTATION

Before that, his short story "All Of Us Are Dying" was adapted by Serling as "The Four Of Us Are Dying." In Johnson's story, a man is seen differently by everyone: each one sees him as the person they desire most strongly to see, which works to his advantage until he meets a man who has harbored murder in his heart for a decade or more. In Serling's adaptation, the man can change his face at will. Matters become complicated and he is killed by an old man who thinks that he is the son who betrayed his family's moral values.

The catch was that the main character was portrayed by four main actors (including Ross Martin of future WILD, WILD WEST fame) as well as several more in a flawlessly executed, single take sequence of him shaving before a mirror.

The next episode, a Serling original, was "The Purple Testament," in which an American officer in Philippines during WWII can see a strange light on the face of those men in his company that are about to die. Following this was "The Monsters Are Due On Maple Street," Serling's tale of suburban paranoia. This tale was the author's statement on Red-baiting and other forms of prejudice common in the Fifties and Sixties. The fact that it does this through the metaphor of alien invaders makes it just as relevant thirty years later.

A fine Charles Beaumont script, "Long Live Walter Jameson," came next. Kevin McCarthy portrayed the title character, a historian who is about to marry the daughter of his older associate, Professor Kittridge. Kittridge spots Jameson's exact double in a book of Civil War photographs, and eventually learns that Jameson is two thousand years old, having achieved immortality through alchemy. Determined to go ahead with the marriage despite Kittridge's strong protests, Jameson gets ready to elope, but is killed by a very old ex-wife who also seeks to stop the wedding. Jameson ages rapidly and fades into dust under Serling's epilogue.

The first season continued with scripts by Serling, Matheson and Beaumont, as well as adaptations including another George Clayton Johnson story, "Execution." The next-to-last episode of the first season, "The Mighty Casey," involved a robot being tested as the new pitcher for a down-and-out baseball team. The team's manager was originally played by actor Paul Douglas, a good actor with a reputation as an ex-drinker. Desmond didn't look too good during shooting, leading all involved to suspect that he had fallen off the wagon. Desmond had actually been undergoing a worsening heart condition, and died mere days after the episode was filmed.

Some shows belong to the stars. A few belong to the writers. Charles Beaumont, Richard Matheson, and Rod Serling owned the TWILIGHT ZONE.

THE SHOW MUST GO ON

On top of this tragedy, the footage of Desmond was unusable due to his obvious physical problems appearing quite clearly on the footage. Eventually, most of the episode was re-shot with Jack Warden as the manager, making as much use of existing footage as possible. The network wouldn't bail out the episode and the cost of the new footage came out of Serling's pocket. THE TWILIGHT ZONE soon garnered considerable awards: Directors Guild and Producers Guild Awards, as well as a Hugo Award! Serling also won an Emmy Award for Outstanding Achievement in Drama.

The second season kicked in with a string of Serling scripts,

23

including another Burgess Meredith outing, "Mr. Dingle, The Strong." Meredith's nebbishy character is granted superhuman strength as an experiment by a two-headed Martian. He uses his powers in such silly ways that the aliens take them away before Dingle can cash in— but then two Venusians decide to give him a leg up by multiplying his intellectual powers by three hundred.

"The Eye of The Beholder" is one of the most famous TWILIGHT ZONE's. A disfigured woman is sent to a ghetto for being deemed *unsightly* by the state. The final twist is that by our standards, she is quite attractive, as is everyone else in the ghetto. The norm of this society is what we would consider hideous.

Matheson checked in with "Nick of Time," where William Shatner becomes obsessed with a fortune-telling machine in a roadside diner. This was followed by Beaumont's "The Howling Man," a great episode where an American traveler refuses to believe monk John Carradine's claim that the prisoner in the abbey is really the devil— until he lets him go and discovers the awful truth—that he has let evil loose upon the world. Another episode, "The Prime Mover," brought George Clayton Johnson back to the Zone; he sold the idea for an unpublished story to scripter Charles Beaumont for six hundred dollars but received no screen credit due to an oversight by the show's producer.

After a few more Serling-penned episodes, Johnson finally debuted with his first script, "A Penny For Your Thoughts." Here, Dick York played a man whose lucky toss of a coin— it lands on its side and stays there— endows him with the ability to read people's minds. He finds, however, that what someone may be thinking does not necessarily mean that they are liable to actually commit that act— a distinction which leads to some poignant humor.

HIGHLIGHTS AND A THIRD SEASON

A real highlight of the second season was Richard Matheson's "The Invaders," starring Agnes Moorehead in a silent struggle against small but deadly invaders from space. Performed largely without dialogue and just with sound effects, we don't discover until the climax that the invaders are actually astronauts from Earth who have landed on a world of giants. One of Serling's best of the season was the Art Carney vehicle "Night Of The Meek." A drunken department store Santa gets a chance to be the real thing. (One viewer objected to having Santa portrayed as a drunkard, but this guy obviously missed the point.) Serling showed that he could indeed still write "serious" stories as the plot dwelt on how miserable Christmas is for the poor and the downtrodden.

The third season had the usual plethora of Serling scripts, as well as George Clayton Johnson's "Nothing In The Dark" (in which Robert Redford plays Death), Charles Beaumont's "The Jungle" (a New Yorker is hunted down by denizens of the jungle he destroyed with an African hydroelectric project), and Johnson's "A Game of Pool" (where Jack Klugman must defeat ghostly poolshark Jonathan

24

Winters in a game for his life.) This season also marked the debut of scripter Earl Hamner, Jr., who would later create THE WALTONS.

A pair of Serling adaptations are real standouts. The first, based on a Jerome Bixby story, was "It's A Good Life," starring Billy Mumy as Anthony, the child who maintains complete control over a small town and wreaks a horrible fate upon anyone who offends him. (This was later remade by Joe Dante in THE TWILIGHT ZONE movie.) The second was based on Damon Knight's "To Serve Man," The title of the story is also the title of the book left by seemingly benevolent aliens—which turns out to actually be a cookbook. Future James Bond nemesis Richard "Jaws" Kiel portrayed one of the towering aliens in this outing.

George Clayton Johnson scored again with another classic episode, "Kick The Can," where an old man portrayed by Ernest Truex learns how to become young again and leads off his retirement-home companions to a literal second childhood. Sadly, his oldest friend is too bitter to accept the notion. Ray Bradbury's "I Sing The Body Electric" was also adapted, by Bradbury himself. This was Bradbury's sole contribution to THE TWILIGHT ZONE, a series which clearly owed much of its inspiration to exactly the type of stories which had launched Bradbury to fame in the Fifties.

THEY CAN'T ALL BE GOOD

There were some clunkers, of course; Serling really fell flat in "The Gift," which is marred by embarrassingly stereotyped por-

trayals of Mexicans. This was offset by the truly fine Serling episode "The Changing Of The Guard," starring Donald Pleasance as an aging schoolteacher convinced that his life has been meaningless—until the ghosts of his students convince him otherwise.

With the advent of the fourth season, THE TWILIGHT ZONE lost both Serling-as-producer (he remained as writer and narrator) and the definite article, becoming merely known as TWILIGHT ZONE. It also became an hour-long show, a move CBS hoped would boost ratings and advertising revenue. What did happen was that the stories were too long and were generally padded out—the strength of the series had been the concise, compact short-story quality that packed a lot of punch in a relatively small package.

Still, there were good scripts; the series kicked off the season with Charles Beaumont's "In His Image," about a disturbed young man who discovers that he is a robot. Another Beaumont script, "Miniature," starred Robert Duvall as a shy man who ultimately finds happiness with the beautiful inhabitant of an antique doll house. Unfortunately, this fine realization of a superb Beaumont script was never syndicated due to a law suit claiming plagiarism by a writer who had submitted a story about store dummies who come to life (obviously the man had never heard of Pygmalion!) The suit was dropped, but "Miniature" was never shown after its initial air date except in recent years in special airings by stations who carry the syndication package of THE TWILIGHT ZONE.

The TWI-LIGHT ZONE was really a series of short stories with a twist ending in the tradition of O. Henry. The science fiction setting allowed more versatility but was otherwise irrelevant.

The rest of the season proceeded with scripts by Serling, Beaumont, Matheson and other writers. The problem with the hour episodes is not (generally speaking) bad story ideas but the fact that the stories generally don't fit the Procrustean time-slot provided by CBS. For strictly commercial reasons, CBS cut TWILIGHT ZONE back to a half hour show when they renewed it for its fifth and final season.

GROWING OLD

In its last season, TWILIGHT ZONE began to show its age, prompting many to suggest that it was beginning to feed on itself. This was frequently true, but even so, the last season included one of the all time classic episodes: Richard Matheson's "Nightmare At 20,000 Feet." Directed by future Superman director Richard Donner, it was a suspenseful drama starring William Shatner as the man who sees a gremlin on the wing of the plane he is riding through a fierce storm. Matheson was quite pleased with it too, even though he didn't care for the monster make-up; he thought that the man who played the creature looked more like his original idea without any makeup on!

This also marked the point at which Jerry Sohl began ghosting scripts for the ailing Charles Beaumont; Beaumont received sole credit on screen, but all of his fifth-season episodes were either co-plotted with Sohl or written completely by Sohl.

The season ended with "An Occurrence At Owl Creek Bridge," a wordless French adaptation of the Ambrose Bierce story. By buying the rights and incorporating this short film as a TWILIGHT ZONE, the show went from being over budget to coming in actually under budget. The film also won the Academy Award.

With the fifth season drawing to a close, CBS did not renew TWILIGHT ZONE. The show's ratings had not really been bad, but Serling himself wasn't terribly interested, and passed on an offer from ABC to do a similar series with a different title. What he had in mind was a proposal for a series he wanted to call "Rod Serling's Wax Museum," but the executive at ABC trying to win Serling over was too keen on having a monster-a-week show like THE OUTER LIMITS, and this notion came to naught.

In a bad business move, Serling sold the rights to the entire TWILIGHT ZONE series to CBS in the Sixties, unwittingly handing over to them vast future syndication profits which he himself should have retained. But work was still available for a writer of Serling's caliber; he won an Emmy in 1964 for a drama he penned for CHRYSLER THEATER, "It's Mental Work."

AN EXTENDED CAREER

Close on the heels of this came another short-lived CBS series, the thoughtful Western series THE LONER, which starred Lloyd Bridges. Serling also worked extensively as a host for television shows, an advertising spokesman, and as a narrator (such as his work for French oceanographer Jacques Cousteau's television documentaries). Various critically acclaimed television scripts followed, as did

1967's PLANET OF THE APES; Serling did three drafts based on Pierre (BRIDGE ON THE RIVER KWAI) Boulle's novel before a final draft, by Michael Wilson reduced the civilization of Boulle's ape-populated world to a more budgetarily feasible primitive level.

A TWILIGHT ZONE situation also befell Serling when his 1966 TV-movie THE DOOMSDAY FLIGHT, about a mad bomber's attempt to destroy a commercial airliner, was aired. This program logged in second in that entire television season's ratings, but it also provoked a rash of copycat bomb threats against practically every major airline. Serling was overwhelmed by this horror, which, happily, consisted only of threats and no real bombs.

In November 1969, the pilot for NIGHT GALLERY was a ratings success for NBC. It featured the directorial outing by a young director named Steven Spielberg. When the series was picked up, Serling declined a production role, and soon found the network boosting the horror on the show. Serling hadn't realized that by not producing the show he would lose creative control. By the time he did, he was contractually obligated to the series. Still, he stuck with it through its two seasons (the first as an hour show, the second season half that), hosting it like THE TWILIGHT ZONE and winning Emmy nominations for "They're Tearing Down Tim Riley's Bar" and "The Messiah of Mott Street." When NIGHT GALLERY was syndicated, it was cut into half-hour segments.

On June 28, 1975, Rod Serling died after a ten-hour heart operation following a heart attack. He left behind a legacy of fantasy that would remain firmly etched on the psyche of generations of American television viewers.

In 1983 TWILIGHT ZONE: THE MOVIE appeared in movie theaters. Produced by Steven Spielberg, the movie presented new versions of "Kick The Can," "It's A Good Life" and "Nightmare at 20,000 Feet," as well as one new story. Unfortunately, the movie did not do the original series much justice.

A TYPICAL NETWORK MOVE

Treating the 1983 movie as something of a pilot, in 1985 CBS chose to revive THE TWILIGHT ZONE as a color, prime time series. What they failed to realize was that by using that title, the audience would be bringing certain expectations to the series which they should have at least attempted to live up to. Instead the producers decided that what Rod Serling had done was "old fashioned" and that since twenty years had passed that they should do something new and different. But audiences didn't want new and different and the ratings seen began to slide. Some excellent shows were done, though, including an adaptation of the Arthur C. Clarke story "The Star," an adaptation of the Robert McCammon story "Nightcrawlers," Harlan Ellison's "Palladin of the Lost Hour" (which won an Emmy), an adaptation of the Stephen King story "Gramma" and the George R.R. Martin story "The Road Less Traveled" about a Vietnam draft dodger who meets his parallel universe self who served in Vietnam—

and whose life was shattered as a result. In spite of wanting to do new and different, the new TWILIGHT ZONE succeeded best when it produced stories more in keeping with the kind of thing Rod Serling had done best in the Sixties.

A *third* version of THE TWILIGHT ZONE was all but sneaked into syndication as, with virtually no fanfare, the color episodes were syndicated along with a couple dozen *new* episodes. But with the almost sole exception of Harlan Ellison's "Crazy As A Soup Sandwich," the made for syndication episodes were pretty thin. The other problem with the syndicated version was that some of the 1985-86 prime time TWILIGHT ZONE episodes were longer than a half-hour, but every story was edited to fit the half-hour slot of the syndication form, including "Palladin of the Lost Hour" which may never be seen in its original broadcast form again.

The new TWILIGHT ZONE of the Eighties failed to capture the imagination or establish a reputation for continuous wonder the way the old Rod Serling series did. People will always remember the on screen presence of Rod in those original episodes and will forever elevate them in the hearts and minds of Serling's legions of fans.

This series is even more closely identified with 60's science fiction than THE TWILIGHT ZONE is. Its frequent use of monsters was a network dictate because that's what most people thought of when they thought of science fiction. In spite of that restriction, the producers tried to deliver more than ordinary fare.

There is nothing wrong with your television set. Do not attempt to adjust the picture. We are controlling transmission. We will control the horizontal. We will control the vertical. We can change the focus from a soft blur and sharpen it to crystal clarity. For the next hour sit quietly and we will control all that you see and hear. You are about to participate in a great adventure. You are about to experience the awe and mystery that reaches from the inner mind to...

The dramatic opening music by Dominic Frontiere established a mood of both wonder and terror which the series then tried its best to deliver. In spite of an uneven quality in both seasons, THE OUTER LIMITS attempted to do on screen what written science fiction often attempted; to tell dramatic tales of human begins which explored the limits of their humanity.

This series was created by Leslie Stevens, who at the time had a series on the air called STONEY BURKE starring Jack Lord. He wanted his company to get more shows on the air and created the concept of a science fiction series called PLEASE STAND BY. The pilot was essentially what we saw later as "The Galaxy Being." Since Stevens anticipated STONEY BURKE being renewed, he hired Joseph Stefano to produce the show, although the pilot had already been completed by then.

Stevens completed the script for "The Galaxy Being" in November 1962 at a budgeted $213,000. Filming began Dec. 3, 1962 at an unused radio station in the Coldwater Canyon area of Los Angeles as well as on the MGM backlot. Dominic Frontiere was in at the beginning, composing the music for PLEASE STAND BY before it was retitled THE OUTER LIMITS. The show was retitled at ABC's behest. The title PLEASE STAND BY sounded too much like an alert, and this was one year after the Cuban missile crisis when people saw a lot of alerts on their TV's. The title briefly underwent a change to BEYOND CONTROL until Stevens settled on the more evocative name THE OUTER LIMITS.

Initially ABC wanted to know who the host would be since THE TWILIGHT ZONE had Rod Serling and ALFRED HITCHCOCK PRESENTS had the man himself up front. To solve this problem Stevens came up with the Control Voice, which was done throughout the series by Vic Perrin, who also provided any needed narration for the stories.

FROM INNER MIND TO
OUTER LIMITS

WE LOVE OUR MONSTERS

When THE OUTER LIMITS premiered on September 16, 1963, it was at the time of the Sixties monster boom. Ergo the powers that be decreed that producer Joseph Stefano include a monster in every episode. Luckily Stefano was talented enough to know how to do this within the realm of eerie and dramatic tales. These monsters became known as "bears." This is actually a term from vaudeville. Whenever a performance was going wrong, they'd send out a comic in a bear costume to liven things up. The series bible Stefano wrote (based on notes by Leslie Stevens) specifically mentions the "bear" and states: "Each play must have a 'BEAR.' The BEAR is that one splendid, staggering, shuddering effect that induces awe or wonder or tolerable terror or even merely conversation and argument." It was decided that the easiest way to do this was by using monsters.

Joseph Stefano had known Leslie Stevens for many years before he was hired to produce THE OUTER LIMITS. His most noteworthy writing accomplishment had been the screenplay adaptation of the Robert Bloch novel PSYCHO for Alfred Hitchcock. It was Stefano's idea that Norman Bates first victim in the film should be an actress who was recognizable but not famous.

Stefano wanted the scripts in THE OUTER LIMITS to stress the human factor in stories. Looking at "The Galaxy Being," which was written and produced by Stevens, one sees that even though it's an interesting story with a lot of imagination, the characters are thin. Visually and imaginatively it's an OUTER LIMITS episode, but emotionally it lacks the power of such episodes as "Architects of Fear" and "The Man Who Was Never Born."

The distinctive look of the first year of THE OUTER LIMITS was largely due to the cinematography of Conrad Hall, who was hand-picked for the job by Leslie Stevens. Hall used techniques more common to movies than television and went on to become one of the top cinematographers in motion pictures.

While Stevens knew how to pick people for their technical skills (he did after all hire Stefano, Hall and Frontiere), it was Stefano who managed to find actors just on the verge of breaking out. Robert Culp, David McCallum and Martin Landau all worked on THE OUTER LIMITS less than three years before starring in their own TV series.

STARTING OUT BIG

Since THE OUTER LIMITS was in black and white, this added to the somber mood required in the often unique dramas the series portrayed. Even so, the budgets for shows were a minimum of $150,000 and often higher, with $40,000 consigned to the budget for the "bear." Although both seasons of OUTER LIMITS presented many fine episodes, the first season was stronger overall and its larger budget really came across on the screen.

The series began with the episode "The Galaxy Being." It concerned Cliff Robertson as a radio engineer who invented a 3-D TV receiver which tunes in on the image of an alien being in the spiral galaxy of Andromeda. By accident, the alien is transmitted to Earth where, through no fault of its own wrecks havoc. It deals with mankind's fear of the unknown, a recurring theme in the series.

The second episode aired was, "The Hundred Days of the Dragon." While eerily effective, it was completely out of step with the rest of the series. It was a political horror story about a Red Chinese agent who murders a presidential candidate and takes his place to become the new leader of the free world. The only science fiction element was a drug which enabled a person to mold their facial features into any form.

The special effects for THE OUTER LIMITS were by Project Unlimited, which also worked with George Pal on such films as THE TIME MACHINE and THE SEVEN FACES OF DR. LAO. Projects Unlimited was founded by Gene Warren, Tim Barr and Wah Chang. "We were in from about the beginning of OUTER LIMITS the first year," Chang recalls. But although Project Unlimited constructed the most memorable monsters seen in that series, they generally didn't design them.

"In the case of OUTER LIMITS, as with most of these TV things, they were very hurried. We would get a rough script and in some cases a lot of the masks had to be fitted to the actor who was wearing it, so we'd have to take a life mask. Sometimes they wouldn't cast the character until a week before they were going to shoot, so you'd be working day and night to get the thing done."

They also had other people working with them like Jim Danforth and a very young David Allen. After Project Unlimited folded, Jim Danforth has done some striking stop-motion work on WHEN DINOSAURS RULED THE EARTH and FLESH GORDON, as well as assisting Ray Harryhausen on CLASH OF THE TITANS. In recent years David Allen formed his own company which provides special effects for motion pictures.

HIGH SUSPENSE

The series really began exercising its potential with "The Architects of Fear," the third episode broadcast. In this story a group of scientists decide that the only way to end the conflict on Earth between nations is to have Earth face a menace of such magnitude that all nations would unite for the common good. They take one of their volunteers (Robert Culp), and through complex surgery change him into an totally non-human being who would seemingly land on Earth and confront the members of the United Nations.

The suspense in this episode is superb, particularly when their plan goes awry and the ship crashlands in a lonely wooded area. The monster starts struggling through the overgrowth, whereupon we see it for the first time, and what a weird thing it is! As interesting a creature as it is, it's not exactly horrific, but in 1964 some television stations actually felt it was a monster not ready for prime time. There were actual cases of stations either blacking out the episode or excising the scenes with the alien and showing them after eleven o'clock at night in order to spare the feelings of those with tender sensibilities.

33

In the episode the creature is never seen head to toe in one shot but rather we see its face, then a glimpse of an arm, and a shot of its legs. The effect is quite weird. Because of the way it was photographed the creature seemed like it couldn't possibly be a man in a suit but seemed like it must be some sort of huge marionette. But Wah Chang has a photograph he took of the costume when it was finished and was being worn by the stuntman. The trick was that the stuntman had to wear the costume while crouching with his hands supported by stilts.

"It was a very difficult thing," Chang confirms," and it really took an athlete to wear this thing. That was worn by stuntman Janos Prohaska. Years later, he and his son and their whole crew were killed in a plane crash. We had a number of actors on OUTER LIMITS who were not well known at that time, like Robert Culp, who went on to become stars."

The drama and the pathos present at the conclusion of the story makes it more than just a monster story as it's also a story about people. This is what made THE OUTER LIMITS so effective in its presentations. Unlike many horror films which build a slight plot with slight characters around some type of monster which abducts women, THE OUTER LIMITS presented firmly constructed stories with believable characters. This, coupled with the moody black and white photography, made for the creation of some genuine classics of the genre. In the one hour format, OUTER LIMITS succeeded in presenting interesting weird fantasies.

REMARKABLE MAKEUP

"The Sixth Finger" presented another remarkable episode which starred David McCallum as a man who has the evolution of his body accelerated by electronics employed on a molecular level. The makeup, which became a byword with excellence on this series, was particularly impressive here as McCallum undergoes several transformations over the course of the hour. It was easily some of the best makeup of its type ever seen on television.

This was followed by "The Man Who Was Never Born," which is the kind of story which THE OUTER LIMITS strived to do in its best moments. This is the one which dealt with an astronaut whose craft pierces the time barrier and lands in a future Earth devastated by a plague. A deformed descendant of humanity explains what happened and accompanies the astronaut in the craft and journeys back into the past to prevent the horrible future. Martin Landau gives a wonderful performance as both the deformed human and as a normal looking man, an appearance he is able to assume using a hypnotic screen. The story deals with love, emotions and ideals, with one of the most disturbing endings of any of the series episodes.

"O.B.I.T." deals with government snooping on private lives, but it's okay because the machine involved unmasks a deadly alien in our midst. It thus skirts over the real issue and misdirects us. "Corpus Earthling," a run of the mill story about alien creatures which look like rocks but can come to life and take over human bodies. Robert Culp is the hero who has a brain operation and then overhears two rocks planning to conquer the Earth. You had to be there.

"Nightmare," on the other hand, has aliens but also a government plot. When an alien device accidentally detonates on Earth, our government takes advantage of this to have war games, but the people involved think the war is real, and some are really killed and maimed. While at the time the concept of a government waging war unnecessarily seemed far-fetched, this was before the Pentagon Papers revealed that this very thing was going on. The episode features a very young Martin Sheen in a pivotal role.

"Tourist Attraction" was another along those lines as it involved a strange sea creature which is captured to be put on display in a South American country to pump up its tourism industry. It is rescued by dozens of its fellow creatures which emerge from the sea.

THOSE CRAZY CREATURES

Some of the strangest creatures ever presented on this series were "The Zanti Misfits." These creatures looked like giant ants with humanlike heads and faces. They're quite bizarre and convincing and were given life via stop-motion animation by Jim Danforth. The story involves the Zanti's sending a ship-load of criminals to Earth because, as it turns out, they *knew* that humans couldn't tolerate such creatures in their midst and would destroy them. A supporting actor in the episode, who's killed off early, is Bruce Dern.

While the monsters on THE OUTER LIMITS were pretty strange, only one came close to looking downright disgusting. That was the creature in the episode "Mice." If people were bothered by the thing in "Architects of Fear," the monster in "Mice" must have really sent them scurrying. The story involves contact with intelligent beings on the planet Chromo. Through teleportation, a human (a convict who volunteers) is to be sent to Chromo while one of the alien race is sent here. When the creature appears, it is so repulsive looking that the volunteer backs out. The somewhat humanoid gelatinous monster has various slimy jutting projections and it injects a food substance (which it grows itself) which looks like soggy bread. A strange one.

One of the weakest first season episodes was "ZZZZZZ." No, that's not a sarcastic comment, that's the title. It concerns a hive of bees materializing the queen bee into the form of a human so that she can lead the bees on a conquest of Earth. Talk about Fifties sci-fi movies!

"The Bellero Shield" features Martin Landau in a supporting role. The story, like many other OUTER LIMITS tales, used science fiction to focus on human weaknesses and character flaws. The plot involves a creature from another world, a world of light, which is captured by the beam of an experimental laser. The creature

> *OUTER LIMITS too often slipped into its familiar monster-of-the-week format, but many stories were very well written.*

35

can encase itself in an impenetrable shield, bell-shaped and transparent, in times of danger.

The lead character is actually Sally Kellerman as Bellero's wife. She kills the creature (or so she believes) and steals its device and plans to exhibit the shield to the world as her husband's invention. While demonstrating it she discovers that she doesn't know how to remove the shield from around her because it is actually operated by the alien's "blood." The alien, before dying, frees her as a parting act of mercy even though she clearly doesn't deserve it. Who is really the monster in this one?

A GRAVE OUTCOME

Fun and games stars the late Nick Adams as a man snatched from Earth and transported to a distant planet and is forced to do battle with an alien. The outcome will decide Earth's fate. It's basically a reworking of the well-known Fredric Brown story "Arena," which STAR TREK did an official adaptation of under that title. Still, THE OUTER LIMITS version is more gritty with some good characterization, giving Nick Adams a good part to chew on. The suspense of the hit-and-run fighting, combined with the anti-hero nature of the Nick Adams character, makes for a much better than average treatment of an otherwise simple idea.

Another episode which holds up well nearly thirty years later is "A Feasibility Study" which has an entire six block residential section of a city transported to the planet Luminos. The people were brought to the planet to test their susceptibility to the disease which infects the planet's inhabitants, making it impossible for them to remain ambient once the infection is complete. If humans prove resistant, more will be kidnapped to establish a race of slaves on the planet. The attitudes of the people captured are carefully scrutinized, with humanity coming out on top when the people decide to deliberately infect themselves to convince the Luminites that Earth is of no use to them, thereby saving countless lives.

There were a number of fine episodes the first season, and another which used the science fiction milieu to make a statement about humanity was "The Chameleon." This starred Robert Duvall as a man who agrees to have his molecular structure altered to impersonate one of the aliens aboard a downed spacecraft in order to gain entry and learn their plans. While he succeeds, the aliens realize that he is not really one of them, but allow his changed body chemistry (brought on by the alien cells used in the structural alteration) to grow in him until he realizes what the aliens are really like. The more the agent "remembers" about their planet, the more he dislikes the grubby creatures of what was once his world. He elects to leave Earth with the aliens.

The final episode of the first season was "The Forms Of Things Unknown," which producer Joseph Stefano did as a pilot for a projected series which would have been called THE UNKNOWN. The story features David McCallum as a man who builds a room in which he can bend time. When THE UNKNOWN didn't make it as a series, the background music was recycled in the Quinn Martin series THE INVADERS.

THE REEL SCOOP

Although some stories have it that THE OUTER LIMITS was canceled and then later renewed, causing the staff of the show to be dispersed and replaced, the reality was much different. Leslie Stevens had been fighting with ABC vice-president Ben Brady's decisions regarding the series all season. Brady would be the first to admit that they didn't get along. Stevens was constantly going over Brady's head to argue with the network over script decisions and it was inevitable that the network would tire of the conflict. Although THE OUTER LIMITS was popular, its rating were not strong and ABC chose to slash the budget for the second season.

Joseph Stefano left the show because ABC switched times-lots, giving the strong Monday night slot he'd been promised to Irwin Allen's more popular VOYAGE TO THE BOTTOM OF THE SEA. Stefano registered his protest by quitting the show. Since Ben Brady didn't care for the distant supervisory position he held at ABC, the network allowed him to vacate the post and return to series production. Brady was recommended for the post of producer on THE OUTER LIMITS and Leslie Stevens took this as a sign that he wasn't wanted either. Thus Stevens had no creative involvement with the second season of the series he created.

Ben Brady came on as producer of THE OUTER LIMITS for its second season. Director of cinematography Conrad Hall, who had contributed much to the look of the first season, was replaced with Kenneth Peach. Brady didn't care for the strange look Hall had brought to the show and wanted something more accessible. The technical people, such as Project Unlimited, remained attached to the show, as did Vic Perrin as the Control Voice. In spite of the restaffing, the second year did produce some very interesting shows, largely due to strong scripts overcoming weak budgets.

Brady was viewed by some as a company man, having stepped into his role straight from the hierarchy of ABC, and yet he found himself battling the network over the same things Stefano and Stevens had. The series budget had been slashed to a top of $100,000 an episode, whereas $150,000 had been the minimum budget per episode in the first season. ABC kept pressuring Brady to include a monster not only in every episode, but early in every episode. Brady felt that this was an artifice which he ignored as much as possible. He wanted good stories and he turned to published science fiction writers whenever possible. Seeleg Lester, the story editor for the second season, stated that the special effects seen in the first year were impossible to do with their new budget. Scripts had to be written with cheapness in mind.

KICKING OFF
THE SECOND SEASON

The first season had used studios at KTTV for filming and headquarters, but for the second season they had to relocate. The new production offices were in a corner of Paramount Sunset, a

37

Often OUTER LIMITS could be very, very good. One example is the premiere episode of the second season, "soldier."

38

bowling alley on Sunset Boulevard which had been reconverted into a soundstage years before by Warner Brothers. New music was written for the second season by Harry Lubin because Dominic Frontiere was too closely associated with the production team from the first season. ABC had endured so many fights with Leslie Stevens that anyone closely associated with him was persona non grata.

The premiere episode of the second season was "Soldier," written by Harlan Ellison. Loosely based on his short story of the same title, the episode deals with a soldier from the future, Quarlo, projected back in time when he's caught in the crossbeams of two laser-type weapons. Captured by police when he loses his helmet, a government investigator cracks the language barrier, determining that Quarlo is speaking a version of English hundreds of years removed from our own.

Quarlo was raised in a "crèche" and never knew a mother or a father—only a "C.O." Lloyd Nolan plays the sympathetic investigator who reaches Quarlo's basic humanity and introduces the trained killer to a world he never knew. Conflicts of character and ideals form the core of the story, which reaches their summit in an explosive climax in which Quarlo seemingly sacrifices his life for his adopted family, only we're left to wonder if it was really as simple as that.

It's a story which holds up well under repeated viewings because it's about something, unlike any episode you can point to from BUCK ROGERS, SPACE: 1999, BATTLESTAR GALACTI-CA, FANTASTIC JOURNEY, LOGAN'S RUN and STARMAN. On television, the level of writing on network science fiction shows has diminished year by year as flash replaced the desire for substance in the stories produced.

Michael Ansara, who was seen often in Sixties television, turned in a performance showing edges of personality so that we would believe that Quarlo was of a different time and place. Lloyd Nolan was effective as Tom Kagan, the philologist, but if his performance seems a little odd that's because he was going deaf and had to read his lines from cue cards.

INSIDE INFORMATION

In THE OUTER LIMITS—THE OFFICIAL COMPANION by David J. Schow and Jeffrey Frentzen (Ace Books, 1986), a page of the shooting script review ABC did for "Soldier" is printed, showing the specific items in the script which the network wanted changed. These include deleting a reference to a toilet as well as cutting any profanity, no matter how mild. For instance it states: If dammeeooo, pp 17 sc 57 - is damn you - DELETE. But the best one is: Page 41, sc 82- The "camp follower - Joy-girl" is good - but unacceptable.

Ellison's original version of "Soldier" is so different from the teleplay version that it could be adapted to television today and only seem slightly similar to the now classic OUTER LIMITS version. Quarlo doesn't die at the end of Ellison's short story, but rather becomes an anti-war lecturer, describing the horrible weapons of combat which soldiers would use against each other in the future. The combat scenes in "Soldier From Tomorrow" (as it was titled in its magazine appearance in 1957) bear an eerie resemblance to some aspects of ground warfare in Vietnam.

"Cold Hands, Warm Heart" followed this thoughtful lead episode, and while it dealt with a human question, it was anything but subtle or complex. When an astronaut (William Shatner) returns from Venus, he begins to undergo a strange transformation until saved by the love of his wife.

"Expanding Human" a couple weeks later is a drug story that deals with a scientist who invents a substance which can temporarily expand his intellect and change his personality. It's an obvious spin on "Dr. Jeykl And Mr. Hyde" but handles the material in an intriguing manner. Keith Andes and Skip Homeier star but co-stars of this episode include James Doohan and Grace Lee Whitney.

By and large the runaway favorite of the second year is "Demon With A Glass Hand," once again scripted by Harlan Ellison who's only other contribution to THE OUTER LIMITS kicked the second season off to a strong start. Starring Robert Culp and directed by Byron Haskin, the show used its budget restrictions largely to its advantage to produce a taut, claustrophobic tale which takes place almost entirely inside a building. This was actually the Bradbury Building located in downtown Los Angeles, a locale also used as the imaginary "Seattle Underground" in the TV movie THE NIGHT STRANGLER.

A REEL KEEPER

The story deals with Robert Culp as a man with a glass hand whose fingers are computer memory banks. It's very swiftly paced as Culp battles aliens who come from the future through a time mirror. Following the teaser, the opening scene under the episode title and credits features Trent (Culp) interrogating an alien prisoner who is bound to the gates of a cemetery in a crucifixion pose.

Arlene (now Tasha) Martel plays a garment worker who was originally written to be Latino, but the network opposed that nationality for the character. Instead she's made Italian with a name that is half-Mexican, and the actress played her as a Latino. She seems to be there as the love interest until the twist at the end shows how we (and she) were misdirected. Robert Culp liked this story so much that for years thereafter he attempted to get backing to turn it into a feature film, something that he still wants to do, only now he would direct rather than star in it.

Three of the glass hands were made by Project Unlimited out of plastic with a small tape recorder in it and other devices to make it look electronic. All three of the props disappeared by the time filming had completed and have not resurfaced since, although Ellison has been attempting to track one down for himself.

The tight budget on the second season shows up with the aliens, whose appearance is altered only by the black circles around the eyes as opposed to the elaborate alien makeups of the first season. Also, a typo made by a secretary who was retyping the script in the

39

Outer Limits production offices changed the word "Sumerian" in the prologue to *"Sumerican,"* which was what was read by Vic Perrin as the Control Voice in the episode.

"The Invisible Enemy" is an effective episode about a spaceship crew on Mars investigating the disappearance of the previous mission on the planet. Even though this is clearly a Fifties sci-fi movie done in one hour form, it's effective as we come to realize that there is *something* deadly living beneath the sands. It's an eerie little scarefest which includes major roles by Adam West and Ted Knight. The direction was once again by Byron Haskin and the script was by science fiction writer Jerry Sohl. The episode was based on a short story of the same title by Sohl which had appeared in the September 1955 issue of IMAGINATIVE TALES.

CREATIVE EFFECTS

Project Unlimited provided the effects using a hand-puppet monster made by Wah Chang. A water tank five feet deep, with ground cork spread over the surface, became the sandy surface of the planet Mars. The Sand-shark puppet was operated from beneath the surface by Paul Pattee. The full scale surface of Mars was constructed in the Paramount stage and covered sixty-five hundred square feet. Stock footage of the spaceship on the surface of (coincidentally) Mars from the film IT! THE TERROR FROM BEYOND SPACE was incorporated as a budget-cutting move. Most of the production crew who worked on the episode considered it to be a real dog and

have been surprised over the years when people have mentioned how much they liked it.

Jerry Sohl was also the co-author of "Counterweight" which concerned a group of people making an important test involving a simulated space flight. Unknown to them, an alien intelligence is also aboard the simulator, an intelligence which wants them to fail so that humanity will be delayed in reaching space. At one point the entity takes over a plant which is aboard and transforms it into a huge, fearsome creature. The excellent transformation is accomplished through stop-motion animation.

The Science fiction writer team of Earl and Otto Binder produced a series of stories under the pseudonym Eando Binder in the 1930's and 1940's, and among their most famous works were the Adam Link stories, tales of a robot which could think like a man. The first of these stories, "I, Robot," was adapted into an episode of THE OUTER LIMITS, although the ending was changed for dramatic purposes. It involves the robot, Adam Link, put on trial for the murder of its creator, although actually the man's death was an accident unrelated to any actions of the robot.

During a recess in the trial, Adam saves the life of a child who would otherwise have been hit by a car. In THE OUTER LIMITS version the robot's body is destroyed, seemingly terminating it. But the head remains intact, and anyone who had read the original stories would have realized that the robot's brain is where its life was housed, its body merely providing a way for it to move around. Leonard Nimoy (who has a small role in the first season episode "The Production and Decay of Strange Particles") plays the pivotal role of the lawyer defending Adam Link, although the robot is actually the main character.

WINDING DOWN

"The Inheritors," the only two-part episode on the series, is a sentimental favorite as it seems to be setting up a menace which turns out to be anything but. The men whose actions seem suspicious and threatening are actually using alien technology to build a spacecraft to take crippled and terminally ill children to a planet where they will remain healthy and live long lives.

The remainder of the episodes, although not bad, were only average—lacking the power and insight which marked the scripts of so many others. "The Brain of Col. Barham" is just another Fifties sci-fi movie done in a one hour format as a human brain kept alive in a laboratory develops super mental powers and threatens humanity.

The final episode, "The Probe," is noteworthy only because it marked the appearance of a creature called the "Mikie," a blob-like thing played by the late Janos Prohaska, a role he repeated with only a slight costume change in the STAR TREK episode "The Devil In The Dark."

The series has continued to be influential. In an interview with STARLOG magazine, James Cameron admitted that THE TERMINATOR was inspired by two OUTER LIMITS episodes. Although Cameron succeeded in getting the quote excised prior to publication of the interview, the cat was out of the bag and it was deter-mined that the two episodes in question were "Soldier" and "Demon With A Glass Hand." Over Cameron's objections, Orion Pictures settled with Ellison out of court and put his name in the end credits of the motion picture, although Cameron recently attempted to get it removed, resulting in Ellison filing a contempt of court action against the writer/director.

THE OUTER LIMITS was a genuine milestone in televised science fiction. As uneven as it may have been, its highs aimed higher more successfully than any science fiction series before it and which no network science fiction series has achieved in the Seventies, Eighties and Nineties.

This was the first intentional outer space science fiction comedy made for television. It's popularity is still on the rise and there's even a brand new comic book series based on the space family Robinson.

This series has taken its lumps over the years, largely because it began as a straightforward, serious adventure show and quickly turned into Dr. Smith's Outer Space Comedy Cavalcade. Sideshow production values on the costumes of the aliens in many episodes didn't help matters. But to those who liked the show, it was wonderful. Above all, it was unique.

The first year of LOST IN SPACE introduced the space-faring Robinson family. It was filmed in black and white which had its advantages. Mainly, it allowed more to be accomplished on a limited budget. Plus shooting special effects in color is much more complicated. But there are other factors involved as well. The cinematography of a black and white show is approached in a very different manner as light and shadow plays a much more important element in the photography.

This was capitalized on to a great degree on LOST IN SPACE that first year, particularly since the settings were other worldly. Since actual exterior shooting for the series was rarely done, and most scenes were filmed on a soundstage, the fact that the stories took place in outer space or on another planet worked to their advantage. While today old black and white shows come across as pretty obvious when an indoor set was standing in for an outdoor locale, on LOST IN SPACE this didn't matter. Another world, even when outdoors, wouldn't be expected to look like our own backyard or the hills north of Los Angeles. And since the Jupiter 2 often landed on fairly arid planets, rocks and sand went a long way in establishing the needed ambiance.

Irwin Allen used the old children's classic Swiss Family Robinson as the inspiration for this, his first television series. He originally planned to call the show SPACE FAMILY ROBINSON but abandoned this because a screenplay by Ib Melchoir was on file with the Writer's Guild with that title. Some sources state that Allen changed the title because Walt Disney Productions had the title Space Family Robinson on file due to the success of their 1960 movie Swiss Family Robinson.

Western Publishing also had a comic book they'd started publishing in 1962 called SPACE FAMILY ROBINSON. When Gold Key comics later licensed LOST IN SPACE for a comic book tie-in, they just added the name to the cover of their SPACE FAMILY ROBINSON comic book, even though any similarities were just superficial at best.

THROWING IT ALL TOGETHER

In a bit of inspired handiwork, Irwin Allen had the Jupiter 2 designed to look like a flying saucer. This went a long way in making the ship look futuristic since the setting of the show was 1997. More than twenty-five years later it allows the show to keep from looking dated. A conventional spacecraft would have made it appear the way Fifties science fiction movies do which used World War Two V-2 look-alikes for their rocket ships.

Casting for this series was reportedly done without a lot of casting calls. June Lockhart was cast after appearing in an episode of VOYAGE TO THE BOTTOM OF THE SEA. She enjoyed working with Irwin Allen and found him to be "dynamic and creative and so in charge of the work."

This original version of LOST IN SPACE was conceived without Dr. Smith and the robot being present in any form. The background music, credited to Bernard Herrmann, is largely just passages taken from the soundtracks of the movies THE DAY THE EARTH STOOD STILL and JOURNEY TO THE CENTER OF THE EARTH. The familiar series music is not present in the original pilot at all and in fact the title theme and end credits are both from THE DAY THE EARTH STOOD STILL. But when the show was revamped and "The Reluctant Stowaway" was produced, all of the music was replaced with the LOST IN SPACE theme music written by "Johnny Williams" (better known today as respected film composer and con-ductor of the Boston Pops Orchestra, John Williams).

Once it was decided to revise the pilot and add Dr. Smith and the robot, a great deal of new footage was used and the pilot was re-edited and spread out over the first five episodes. Only one brief scene, a shot of Alpha Control, appeared in episode two, "The Derelict," which was otherwise completely new.

Some footage appeared only in "No Place To Hide." For instance, even though the spaceship encounters a meteor storm in both the pilot and in "The Reluctant Stowaway," this footage was refilmed for the opening episode of the series. A view of the swirling meteor storm seen through the viewport of the spacecraft appears only in "No Place To Hide." The logbook and John Robinson's voiceovers, which are quite effective in the pilot, do not appear at all in "The Reluctant Stowaway" or any other series episodes.

FILMED BUT NEVER USED

The other scenes not reused from "No Place To Hide" are relatively minor. For instance, a shot of Debby the Bloop standing on the Chariot's radar scope playing with John, as well as a couple lines of dialogue John Robinson has in the Chariot during their trip in the storm are edited out of the revised version of the story.

The most interesting unused scene from "No Place To Hide" is the final one where the Robinsons have reached the tropics and are giving thanks. As they silently pray (all of them kneel except for Donald West, who stands but bows his head), two large-headed aliens are secretly observing the family from behind some bushes. One alien looks at the other and nods his head. But while this scene never appeared in the series as it was broadcast, it did appear in a sixty second promo for LOST IN SPACE which CBS ran during its first season on the air, as well as in advance of its 1965 fall premiere.

One problem in the original pilot was that it stated both that the spacecraft would be traveling at the speed of light and that it would take 98 years to reach Alpha Centauri. What they fail to mention (and which most children learn in high school astronomy) is that Alpha Centauri is only four light years away. This was corrected in "The Reluctant Stowaway" so that the voyage was postulated as taking just over five years, which made much more sense.

In "The Reluctant Stowaway," both the robot (called an environmental control robot) and Dr. Smith are introduced in the same sequence. There is also new footage filmed showing interaction before takeoff between the Robinsons and Dr. Smith. In fact when the family receives their final pre-liftoff checkups, the shadowy figure speaking to them is revealed to be Dr. Smith, the saboteur we'd first met just minutes earlier. The villainy of Smith is emphasized when he casually watches the Robinson family board the Jupiter 2 after he's sabotaged the robot with new programming. The robot is scheduled to destroy the ship's controls eight hours into the mission. So Smith is watching the family

leave in the firm belief that they'll all die hours later. What a fun guy.

It's never made clear what the point of the sabotage is. While the narrator says that certain foreign powers want to see the mission fail, we're never told why. The only gain that the Jupiter 2 mission stands to make is for the benefit of all humanity, not for the benefit of any one nation.

Irwin Allen used the old children's classic Swiss Family Robinson as the inspiration for this, his first television series.

BUSDRIVER IN SPACE

While Donald West was called Dr. Donald West in the original pilot and had been given a pile of scientific credits, in the revised episode he's Major Don West and is just meant to be their pilot and is along to operate the ship should it malfunction. When Dr. Smith is trapped aboard the ship, he finally accepts his situation and straps himself in to the seat which had somehow been hidden inside a control panel of the ship. When the Jupiter 2 takes off, Smith screams either in pain or terror or both.

In "No Place To Hide," the meteor swarm the ship encounters was uncharted and caught everyone by surprise. In "The Reluctant Stowaway" it is supposedly Smith's extra mass on the ship which prevents the electronic brain from responding and automatically steering the Jupiter 2 out of harm's way.

Watching "No Place To Hide" and "The Reluctant

45

Stowaway" back to back is an odd experience because they are largely two completely different treatments of the same idea. The addition of Dr. Smith and the robot creates a completely new dynamic in the show. In the original version of LOST IN SPACE there was no irritating influence. The story is purely about the adventures of the Robinsons and how they deal with the challenges of being on their own on an alien world. It's one adventure after another and we see how the family deals with it. Even Donald West is very much a part of the family.

The insertion of Dr. Smith fractures that. He divides them and creates disharmony. After the family is revived from suspended animation, Maureen Robinson is all for returning to Earth. But John Robinson is against that and prefers to leave that decision up to the computer. Maureen questions this since she feels that her family is threatened by what has happened. She even asks Dr. Smith whether in some people it takes longer for the heart to thaw from freezing. This is not the happy family we saw in "No Place To Hide."

Jonathan Harris was cast after his agent was contacted by Irwin Allen's office and asked to send over some footage of the actor at work. Harris refused, wanting to know first what kind of performance they wanted to see, lest he supply a sample of a dramatic performance when they were thinking of casting him in a comic role. Harris finally said he'd prefer to meet the producer in person. Allen was furious. He contacted Jonathan's agent and said, "Who the hell does he think he is, and I'll

see him at four o'clock!" Harris was cast at that same meeting, without reading for the part.

THE VOICE

Narration done by the Alpha Control TV commentator is the voice of Don Forbes, who provided similar duty on VOYAGE TO THE BOTTOM OF THE SEA. In the original pilot, "No Place To Hide" (which was never broadcast in that form), only Forbes as the announcer is heard. In the actual first aired episode, "The Reluctant Stowaway," some of the announcing by Forbes is replaced when new narration was added by Dick Tufeld (who was also the voice of the robot).

Dick Tufeld first met Irwin Allen years before LOST IN SPACE. Tufeld was eighteen and attending Northwestern University in Chicago in the early Forties when he had his first encounter with Irwin Allen, who was then working in radio. "My home was in Los Angeles and I came back home one summer and got a job at KLAC radio working summer relief as an announcer. Part of our duties was to spin records and be engineers at the station. There was a guy there who had a Hollywood gossip type show and that was Irwin Allen! I used to spin his theme music and announce the opening of the show and that's when I first met him. He must have been in his late twenties then."

Years later, their paths would cross again. "I had a good friend named Emmet Lavery who was working in the business affairs department at 20th Century Fox. He knew Irwin and they were talking one day and Irwin mentioned to him that he was looking for a narra-

46

tor for his new series, LOST IN SPACE. Emmet suggested me and I think that Irwin vaguely remembered me. I was working at ABC at the time, but that's how I got called in for the show." After trying out for the narrator, and being accepted for that position, Dick tried out for the voice of the robot. Interestingly enough, Dick had also been the narrator on Guy Williams' previous TV series, Zorro.

"After the first episode of LOST IN SPACE was being put together I got a call from my agent. He said that there was a robot character on the show now and Irwin was looking for a voice for it. I guess he wasn't satisfied with Bob May, who was inside the robot, so he said that he'd like me to read for it. I showed up at the scheduled time at Fox, in one of the audio rooms. I remember the first thing I said to Irwin was, 'This is a robot so I presume what you're looking for is a kind of mechanical, robotian kind of sound?' Irwin recoiled and looked at me with horror and said, 'My dear boy, that is precisely and exactly what I do not want. What we have here is a very advanced, civilized culture and what I want is a low key, laid back Alexander Scourby kind of approach.'

GIVE HIM WHAT HE WANTS?

Well, that was a great New York narrator and actor who has since passed away and who did many wonderful documentary narrations and who was very cultured and laid back. So I started reading for him doing my best Alexander Scourby kind of imitation and he would say no, you're not getting it,

try again. After about ten minutes Irwin said, 'Well, this is not working. I appreciate your coming in, but you're still the narrator on the show and we'll see you later.' So I said, 'Irwin, let me try one more thing for you,' and I said something like 'Warning! Warning! Danger! It will not compute!' in my best mechanical, robotian kind of sound.

Irwin said, 'My God! That's that Alexander Scourby approach I wanted! What the hell took you so long?' Honest, I had to turn away from him because I was afraid I was going to laugh in his face, and I couldn't have explained what I was laughing about! Like all of us, Irwin said what he wanted, but what he really wanted was what sounded right to his ear. He described what he wanted, but when I gave it to him it didn't sound right to his ear. When he heard a kind of mechanical robot sound, that sounded right in spite of what he said to me."

Inside the robot was Bob May, who wore the suit all three seasons. He'd speak the robot's lines in order to maintain the timing of a scene, and Dick Tufeld would loop the dialogue later doing the robot's voice that we're all familiar with now. The robot was designed by Robert Kinoshita, who had also designed Robbie the Robot for the 1956 film FORBIDDEN PLANET.

While everyone remembers the Robinson's forever marooned on a planet where they have their adventures, the Jupiter 2 doesn't actually land on a planet until episode three, "Island In The Sky," (which is almost the same identical title as an old Arthur C. Clarke novel, ISLANDS IN THE SKY). While shooting with the actors was

47

LOST IN SPACE ranged from the almost sublime to the totally ludicrous. Perhaps the invasion of vegetables was the worst; vegetarians beware!

generally done indoors, special effects showing the miniature Jupiter 2 model crash-landing on the planet was done in California's Red Rock Canyon near the Mojave Desert. Considering the barren nature of the unnamed planet they crash on, the setting was perfect.

MOST MEMORABLE

Episode four is one of those most people remember because it has the scene with the giant which John Robinson shoots with the laser. As in many pilots, the drama and the special effects were more ambitious than what the tight shooting schedule of a regular series could normally allow. The giant, seen in episode four, had a costume which was actually constructed from dried palm fronds. The suit was designed and constructed by Paul Zastupnevich and is quite effective. While Dawson Palmer is often credited as having played the giant, the credits for "No Place To Hide" (the name of the original pilot for which the footage was originally shot) state that it was played by Lamar Lundy. Dawson Palmer appeared in a character part in the later first season episode "The Space Croppers."

The Bell Rocket belt was employed in these early episodes since it was a science fiction-type device which really worked and captured the imagination of everyone who'd ever seen it used. You believed a man could fly! The most amazing thing about the suit is that further research and development on it was discontinued as the version of it which exists today is little different from the one unveiled to the public in the early sixties. The suit was also used in the James

Bond movie THUNDERBALL in 1964.

In the beginning, Dr. Smith wasn't just conniving, he was nasty and his personality had an edge that made him seem dangerous. In episode one, he knocks out a guard and dumps him down a waste disposal chute. But already by episode eight he's started whimpering and is quite different from the self-assured saboteur seen in the pilot. Jonathan Harris takes credit for this change in direction of the character, having chosen to play his character more like a petulant child than a cold hearted villain. He believed that a straight villain would have proved boring after a short time. Whether he's correct on this point continues to receive mixed reviews from some fans.

This is particularly true in light of the fact that many episodes became outright comedies which emphasized Dr. Smith, the robot and Will Robinson to the exclusion of everyone else. Some fans who haven't seen the show in a long time incorrectly recall that the entire first season was more dramatic with the second season introducing the silly stories. In actuality, the style of the series had largely emerged by halfway through the first season and it seldom deviated from that course.

EVERYTHING IS REUSABLE

The lighter touch to stories began in earnest in episode six, "Welcome Stranger," in which Warren Oates in his best cowboy tradition portrays Jimmy Hapgood, the runaway astronaut. Hapgood claims to have launched from earth on June 18th, 1982 bound for a soft landing on Saturn—but he missed.

Footage of his spacecraft liftoff, as well as the craft itself, would turn up again and again in the series. It was unusual for Irwin Allen to use something only once, as his constant use of stock footage from his film THE LOST WORLD proves. Footage from that film was used in both VOYAGE TO THE BOTTOM OF THE SEA (extensively) and TIME TUNNEL.

While the characterization of Dr. Smith became fairly thin and repetitious after a few episodes, one of his last interesting serious character scenes occurs in episode five, "The Hungry Sea." When he discovers that a heat wave is coming, he sends the robot out to warn the Robinsons of the danger they'll be in when the planet nears the sun should the family not be near any shelter at the time.

If you have a large enough screen which doesn't crop the picture at the edges the way smaller TV screens do, an on-screen blooper can be seen in episode eight, "Invaders From The Fifth Dimension." In the finale, as the robot walks past rocks and bushes towards the alien ship, the legs of Bob May (the man in the robot suit) can be seen. This is because the robot suit was cumbersome and when it had to move, if it was possible to shoot the robot from the waist up only, then May would wear only the top part of the robot. We saw the actual way the suit could be disassembled into pieces in those episodes where the robot had supposedly been blown apart or taken apart by someone.

The upper and lower decks of the Jupiter 2 were on separate sound stages. But in episode nine, "The Oasis," Maureen Robinson enters the elevator on the lower deck and seemingly in one shot travels to the upper deck. Skillful directing by Sutton Roley made this possible.

We get to see one of the special effects miniatures of the Jupiter 2 in episode eleven when Dr. Smith tries to create a duplicate of the ship with his wishing machine, but the machine cannot recreate something that large. Speaking of reusing things, the diving bell used in VOYAGE TO THE BOTTOM OF THE SEA becomes the Jupiter 2's reactor chamber in episode twelve.

CONTINUITY

A dog is introduced in episode thirteen which plays an important role but is never seen again. But then the lost civilization in episode twenty-seven is left sleeping in caverns below the surface and they aren't mentioned again, even in passing, when the Jupiter 2 flees the exploding planet in the opening episode of season two. The continuity on the series wasn't bad, but it wasn't without holes here and there. In season two they meet a hermit on one of the worlds they land on. When they later flee that world as it's about to be destroyed by a comet, no one wonders whether the hermit will be all right.

In spite of the large regular cast, LOST IN SPACE was no more a true ensemble show than STAR TREK was. But while STAR TREK featured its three top lined performers in each episode, LOST IN SPACE featured the performers who had secondary billing in the starring parts. Jonathan Harris was listed as the "Special Guest Star" for all three seasons (his idea), while Billy Mumy was a co-star and the robot had no billing at all. But these three clearly starred in most of the stories. Guy Williams, who had starred in Walt Disney's ZORRO in the late fifties, as well as a couple feature films, reportedly chaffed at seeing himself getting star billing while the scripts made him a supporting character circling the focal point of Dr. Smith and Will Robinson. People who wrote for the series reported that Williams threw what they described as "temper tantrums" on the set over the way his character was shunted aside.

The growing importance in the storylines of Billy Mumy was particularly emphasized in episode fifteen, "Return From Outer Space," where the main plot dealt with Will being transported back to Earth where no one will believe that he's who he claims he is. It's actually one of the better shows. Had Billy Mumy not been up to the acting demands, the scripts wouldn't have continued to feature him. The town Will appears in, Hatfield Four Corners, was just a street set on the backlot of 20th Century Fox. What always struck me as odd about that episode was that even though this town was supposed to be in the year 1997, nothing about it seemed any more modern than 1966. It was as though they were saying that in thirty years, nothing would really change at all! It was just a typical, rural country village. Everything in it was ordinary, including the school buses and the telephone Will uses. Will Robinson doesn't even seem to find this unusual.

When Michael Rennie guest starred in "The Keeper," it was a reunion for him and Jonathan Harris as the two actors had starred in the short-lived Fifties television series THE THIRD MAN. Various props from other episodes turn up in this show, including the derelict ship model from the second episode. A giant spider used in this episode was used later on another Irwin Allen series when it became a giant underwater spider in VOYAGE TO THE BOTTOM OF THE SEA.

A FAMOUS GUEST STAR

Episode twenty, "War Of The Robots," guest starred a player from the stable of Metro Goldwyn Mayer. Robby the Robot, who had appeared in the movies FORBIDDEN PLANET and THE INVISIBLE BOY, turns up as the evil robotoid. The Robinsons apparently found a trunk they hadn't unpacked yet as they're wearing new uniforms beginning in this episode.

By episode twenty-four, "His Majesty Smith," the format of the show was solidly in place as story after story revolved around Smith. This episode was the first time that a Smith lookalike would be used and it would by no means be the last.

Irwin Allen's penchant for using something from one series over on another that he was producing really became obvious in "The Lost Civilization" (episode twenty-seven) when the interior sets of the Seaview did double-duty as the super-scientific underground kingdom sets. The diving bells from the Seaview turn up in the following episode, "A Change of Space," as alien spacecraft. The alien in the same episode also turned up on an episode of Voyage as a Man-Fish. So the two shows definitely traded props and suits back and forth.

The final episode of season one actually featured John Robinson as the focal character. He's possessed by an alien mask which causes him to be harsh to his family and even threaten them. The story is meant to demonstrate the depth of feeling that family members have for one another. Kanto orders John Robinson to kill his son but Robinson is able to overcome the alien's influence. In spite of some scenes with Smith, much of it hearkens back to the style of the first four episodes of the series.

Color came to outer space in the second season of the series. STAR TREK also joined the television lineup a week before the second season premiere of LOST IN SPACE and the two series have been compared to one another ever since. It's inescapable even though the two shows are really quite different in their approach. The only thing they have in common is that both shows take place on other planets and beyond our solar system. The two shows did have one other connection at the time. In "The Cave of the Wizards" (episode fifty-one) Dr. Smith briefly gets pointed ears, which were props acquired from the Star Trek production staff.

CUTTING CORNERS

In "Wild Adventure" they actually get into contact with Alpha Control again but for convoluted reasons they supposedly cannot return to Earth at that time because the sun is between them and the Earth. Also, they're low on fuel. An alien bird-man which appears in "Forbidden World" (episode thirty-three) wasn't borrowed from any other Irwin Allen production. Instead it was a costume used by the late Janos Prohaska in the "Amusement Park" episode of OUTER LIMITS and in the original STAR TREK pilot "The Cage."

Continuity comes into play again in episode thirty-five, "The Prisoners Of Space" in which aliens (stock Irwin Allen monster costumes) put the Robinsons on trial for crimes they inadvertently committed in space. In the case of Dr. Smith, his crimes were deliberate, such as his attack on a creature in episode two. Another of that race of creatures is one of the judges. Trial evidence consists of black and white footage from the first season of the show.

Irwin Allen was notorious for cutting corners. in "The Golden Man" director Don Richardson needed a spacecraft which would have cost $10,000 to construct. Allen wouldn't hear of it. Instead he raided the studio prop department and found a giant plastic champagne glass used in an old Marilyn Monroe film. By turning the prop upside down and putting a newly constructed frame around it, he had the needed alien spacecraft.

Considering that they were on alien worlds, the Robinsons kept encountering situations straight out of terrestrial folklore. In "The Questing Beast" a knight pursuing a dragon shows up. In another episode the Robinsons encounter the gods of Norse mythology. They even encounter ancient Arabian counterparts. Alien mythology doesn't manage to turn up. Everything which does is some

LOST IN SPACE proved successful to spawn toys, g a m e s , books, and c o m i c books. Now, almost thirty years later, there is still a comic book series.

form of a familiar Earth situation, such as a department store or a toy shop. It's because of things like this, and the fact that Will Robinson is often a central character, that some people regard LOST IN SPACE as a children's show.

When a series is successful enough to spawn toys, sometimes that series can turn around and take advantage of that. This is exactly what LOST IN SPACE did in "The Mechanical Men" in which a horde of tiny robots, which look just like the Robinsons' robot, besiege the family. By taking a lot of the Remco toy robots then available in stores, and spray-painting them silver, they had a cheap source of tiny duplicate robots. Today those toys are collector's items and it would be difficult to find that many toy LIS robots.

FAMILIAR NAMES

Actor John Carradine appeared in a couple Irwin Allen series. Having worked in motion pictures since the thirties, his name was quite well known. All too often on TV shows he was reduced to playing some sort of ersatz Shakespearean role or something else which required him to deliver dialogue in an arch and archaic manner. But in the final episode of year two on LOST IN SPACE he played an alien on the lam who assumes human form in order to freely associate with humans. Carradine also appeared in an episode of LAND OF THE GIANTS.

Robert Duncan also worked on a number of Irwin Allen shows, including THE TIME TUNNEL and LOST IN SPACE. In the October 1991 STARLOG, Duncan

described what it was like working on LOST IN SPACE and described what it was like visiting the set and writing for the series with his wife, Wanda, during the second and third season. "I remember Jonathan Harris serving cookies to Wanda's mother when she visited the set; June Lockhart, who was never other than even-tempered, sweet and professional; Guy Williams and his tantrums; Billy Mumy riding his bike around; and the one episode where our guest-star showed up skunk-drunk and stayed that way through all the days he worked. Being drunk gave him a swagger and character he wouldn't have had sober, and he did his lines perfectly."

Regarding the third year of the series, Duncan explained that the writers were definitely told to take a different approach. "We were told that there had been too much whimsy in the second year, and we were instructed to follow new guidelines for LOST IN SPACE's third year. The result was a season with fewer scenes between family members, less interplay between Dr. Smith and the Robot, and more action. It was far easier to write action than whimsy. Irwin was definitely action-oriented, while [SPACE story editor] Anthony Wilson was a very whimsical man. One of the shows Tony wanted to do was our take-off on Tarzan, with the chimp being the intelligent being who provides all the brains for a very dumb Tarzan. That would have been filmed, had LOST IN SPACE continued."

When the Robinsons and company returned for their third and final season, they were sporting new uniforms again. Any time they change costumes like this, no mention is ever made in the storyline where they suddenly appeared from. Just as in the season two opener, they have to leave the planet quickly due to imminent disaster. In this case the crisis is an approaching comet which is going to strike the planet (actually stock footage from a Time Tunnel episode). Robby the Robot appears in this episode again but no one mentions his striking resemblance to the evil robotoid they encountered when reality was black and white.

ENOUGH IS ENOUGH

By this time Guy Williams had become pretty fed up with the constant parade of Dr. Smith/robot/Will Robinson stories. Producers promised a change in direction in the third season and at first that seemed to be the case. The stories were more well balanced among the performers in the first couple episodes and Guy Williams had more to do. There was even a promise made to do stories featuring the other characters more prominently, such as in the first season when Penny was the focal point of a couple episodes.

The second episode of this season ("Visit To A Hostile Planet") indicated positive things ahead. The Jupiter 2 actually returns to Earth. The fact that it's Earth in the year 1947, fifty years before they were launched certainly presented its share of problems. Primarily, though, the story is not played for the drama otherwise inherent in the situation. The most interesting thing in the story is the actual exterior shooting (as opposed to being bound inside a soundstage) and the Jupiter 2 full size mockup equipped with its little seen landing gear.

The third season also introduced the space pod, a story device never seen before. It's certainly useful and no explanation of where it has been hiding up until then is even attempted. On the other hand, Star Trek did much the same thing when after a few episodes of the first season they suddenly introduced the shuttlecraft, something which would have proven vital in solving a dilemma in an episode just a couple weeks before. But STAR TREK wasn't bound to a strict set of circumstances like LOST IN SPACE where the Robinsons and crew were forced to rely on only what was in the Jupiter 2 when it was launched. Introducing a whole new function of the spacecraft after two years on the air is hardly making changes during its early formative period.

LOST IN SPACE borrows more stock footage from itself in "The Haunted Lighthouse" (episode sixty-six) by reusing footage of a space station from the second season show "Wild Adventure." "Flight Into The Future" comes up with some interesting ideas and uses them effectively. We see a rusted out version of the Jupiter 2 and the story is more involved than usual. The space suits seen in this episode had been seen before by Irwin Allen fans on an episode of THE TIME TUNNEL.

PASSING THROUGH

Daniel J. Travanti, of Hill Street Blues fame, guest-starred in the 1967 LOST IN SPACE episode "Collision Of Planets" (episode sixty-eight) as the leader of a group of alien bikers! Episode seventy-two ("Two Weeks In Space") guest stars an actress named Edy Williams. Although not well known today, many fans actually see her every year when an annual event, The Academy Awards, is broadcast. In an obvious bid for self-promotion, Edy Williams shows up at the Oscars every year so that she can parade around for the cameras in some outlandish costume certain to make the late news broadcasts. Alien spacecraft stock footage used in this episode is courtesy WAR OF THE SATELLITES, a Roger Corman drive-in movie from the fifties.

The Jupiter 2 returns to Earth without most of the Robinsons in "Target: Earth" (episode seventy-five). It's an interesting story in which most of the actors are called upon to play inhuman imitations of themselves, and the result is quite effective. The black and white footage of the Jupiter 2 encountering a meteor storm back in the pilot episode is reused here and is tinted to try to make it pass for color footage. It works well enough.

Sheila Mathews (the future Mrs. Irwin Allen) turns up in another LOST IN SPACE episode when she appears in "Princess Of Space," episode seventy-six. Sheila appeared in a number of Irwin Allen shows in guest-star roles, as well as in some of his movies, including THE POSEIDON ADVENTURE and THE TOWERING INFERNO.

Another very good third year episode is "Time Merchant." Bob and Wanda Duncan were regular contributing writers to Irwin

Allen shows and their script for this one is quite inventive. When Dr. Smith escapes back through time, he actually becomes himself in the hours before the Jupiter 2 is set to launch in 1997. In yet another twist, we learn that had Smith not sabotaged the Jupiter 2, that it would have been destroyed by an uncharted asteroid while the Robinsons were in suspended animation. Black and white footage from the pilot is used on a monitor screen, and continuity is actually followed in that the pre-takeoff sequences in 1997 featuring the robot have it speaking in its unemotional monotone from the early episodes before the voice became more personalized.

Judy Robinson actually gets the rare spotlight in "Space Beauty" (episode eighty). Even though Judy and Major West seemed to be pairing off early in the series, her character kept getting pushed into the background and all but forgotten. It was only fair that she be featured at least once in awhile.

VEGETABLES WILL NEVER BE THE SAME

"The Great Vegetable Rebellion" remains perhaps the most infamous episode of LOST IN SPACE. Even Bill Mumy has dubbed it the worst episode in the series. Actually it's one of those stories that's so bad it's good. Seeing Dr. Smith being turned into a giant stalk of celery is too strange for words. Stanley Adams as a human carrot is just plain silly. One has to wonder what possessed Peter Packer to write this episode. The final episode of the series, "Junkyard In Space" isn't bad, but it would've been more fitting had

"Time Merchant" been the series finale.

There has been a rumor floating around LOST IN SPACE fandom for many years that a fourth season episode titled "The Secret of the Jupiter 2" was filmed just before the series was canceled. This rumor is false. Had such an episode existed, even if it hadn't aired after the third season of the show went off the air, it would have become part of the syndication package. LOST IN SPACE was created to make money for its owners. Letting an episode sit on the shelf when it could be sold into syndication makes no sense. When Beauty And The Beast was canceled, there were some unaired episodes which existed, but they were quickly sold as part of the syndication package and aired on the Lifetime channel.

The fact that there were unbroadcast episodes actually made the syndication package that much more attractive. While it's rare for a series to shoot episodes for the following year at the end of the current production season, it's not impossible and has in fact been done from time to time. Usually this happens when there's a threatened strike on the horizon of actors or writers. But this wasn't true of LOST IN SPACE. And if there had been an unseen episode, one or all of the cast members would have mentioned it sometime in the past twenty years.

Several years ago, Billy Mumy wrote a script for a LOST IN SPACE reunion film. He had Twentieth Century Fox interested, but Irwin Allen refused to even discuss it or even look at the script. He told Mumy that if the show were

ever revived that he (Allen) would write it. The project collapsed after that.

The plot of Billy Mumy's proposed reunion show, which he titled "Epilogue," was as follows. Some fifteen years have passed and the Robinsons are still marooned on the last planet they landed on. There's no dutronium on the planet and so no way to refuel the spacecraft. The hardships of living on the planet for fifteen years has created some rifts in the family. The Jupiter 2 has been turned into separate dwellings for everyone. Don has married Judy and they have a son, who hangs around with Dr. Smith.

TOUGH TO SELL

Meanwhile, Will is attempting to discover a substitute power source for the Jupiter 2. When a small spacecraft crashes on the planet Dr. Smith and the boy find it. This unites everyone in an effort to cannibalize the wrecked spacecraft in the hopes of finding a way to use it to power the Jupiter 2. They manage to get the Jupiter 2 running again, but just as they're going to take off, another alien ship arrives. This is the mothership of the small craft which had crashed.

The crew of the smaller craft had been killed in the crash, but when the aliens discover that the Robinsons had plundered the crashed ship, they believe the family to be pirates. The aliens destroy both the robot and the Jupiter 2 and take them prisoner. The aliens take the Robinsons to a space station where there are representatives of every alien race. The misunderstanding is finally worked out, the robot is recreated and the Robinsons are allowed to return to

55

Earth, bringing the saga of LOST IN SPACE to a happy resolution.

Irwin Allen's first complaint to any resolution of the series was that he believed that it would undercut interest in the series since it would have an ending. People would know how it turned out. But on the other hand, how satisfying can it be to watch an old series which you know has no resolution? After awhile it seems pointless. Also, reportedly Allen didn't want to have to resort to doing a sequel to an old project, but wanted to continue to prove himself by doing new things.

He'd made a sequel to THE POSEIDON ADVENTURE called BEYOND THE POSEIDON ADVENTURE which had bombed badly and tarnished his image as a producer, coming as it did directly on the heels of another flop he produced called THE SWARM. Irwin Allen's last produced project had been the 1986 TV musical adaptation of Alice In Wonderland. He hadn't made anything after that and in 1990 had actually reconsidered the idea of a LOST IN SPACE reunion film following market research which indicated that there was a lot of interest in seeing one. He'd even scheduled a meeting with Twentieth Century Fox to discuss it but his failing health had forced him to cancel the meeting. Several months later, Allen died.

While science fiction on television certainly didn't begin with

STAR TREK, everything which has come along since has been mea-

sured by it, including several of the other series covered in this book.

In the 1991 celebrations surrounding the twenty-fifth anniversary of STAR TREK, little note was made of the fact that the international debut of the show occurred two days earlier than the official date. On September 6, 1966, STAR TREK premiered on Canadian television. It was a full two days later that the American premiere took place on NBC. The episode aired was not the pilot (that was shown two weeks later) but the sixth episode filmed, "Man Trap."

The choice of this tale to kick things off was a wise one. "Man Trap" included the three leading characters who would come to mean STAR TREK for generations to follow.

First in order of creation was the character of Spock, Gene Roddenberry's logical alien, who had been part of the original series concept back when the captain of the Enterprise had been, in Gene's mind, one Robert April. Spock served under one other captain before the helm was passed to the third, most famous one, James T. Kirk.

The third character, Dr. Leonard "Bones" McCoy, would not have been in on things from the start if the episodes had been aired in the order in which they were filmed. It was fitting that this seemingly cynical but strongly compassionate humanitarian, who would provide a constant counterpoint to the cold logic of Spock, should be on hand for the first broadcast of STAR TREK. With him on board, STAR TREK was launched.

"Man Trap" featured Dr. McCoy's apparent reunion with his old flame Nancy, now married to archaeologist Robert Crater. Unfortunately, Nancy is actually dead and is being impersonated by a shape-shifting creature that lives off the body salt of other living creatures. Although on the surface a "monster" story, the salt vampire is actually an intelligent being capable of conversing with humans.

THE REAL THING

The third episode broadcast, "Where No Man Has Gone Before," was in fact the pilot that had sold NBC on the series. This episode had been filmed beginning on July 21, 1965 and had taken six months to finish, at a cost of $330 thousand. (The standard per-episode budget would be set at about 180 thousand.) The STAR TREK of this pilot was different from the form that it would soon assume. Uhura had not yet joined the roster, nor had Yeoman Janice Rand. The ship's doctor, Dr. Piper, was portrayed by Paul Fix; and Sulu was a physicist, not the helmsman. Several characters in key roles appeared only in the pilot and, as noted, Dr. McCoy was nowhere to be seen. To further

feed the mania of future trivia enthusiasts, Kirk's middle initial was given as "R" is this episode!

The show really began to hit its stride with "The Naked Time," which gave the STAR TREK cast a chance to show off their range when an alien microbe opened up the ship's crew to their innermost personal conflicts. Kirk's love of the Enterprise warred with his knowledge that his command kept him from having a normal life. Spock's dual heritage led to even more divided behavior, and he was seen to actually weep. This solo Spock scene was actually written by Nimoy and they were barely able to fit filming of it into the schedule.

STAR TREK can be credited with many things—who would have believed, in 1966, that so many terms and phrases from the series would work their way into common parlance? STAR TREK also was the first show to use the by-now-dreaded cliché of the evil twin— a device used countless times since to give a series star more time on screen. In the case of STAR TREK's pioneering use of this plot trick, "The Enemy Within" escaped when a transporter malfunction divided Kirk into two diametrically opposed selves.

William Shatner, allegedly hungry for time on-camera, made the most of this concept. He was duplicated again in the episode "What Are Little Girls Made Of?" Shatner would again get to play a duplicate of himself in the third season episode "Whom Gods Destroy" when Kirk faced off a shape-shifting madman— and, twenty-five years later, in STAR TREK VI, he'd still be at it!

In another first, the Enterprise wound up in dire need of fresh dilithium crystals in "Mudd's Women," one of the three scripts proposed for the second pilot submission, which also introduced Roger C. Carmel as the rascally space swindler Harry Mudd.

MINDS MELD

The Vulcan mind meld, which conveniently served as a means of avoiding a lengthy expository conversation with a mentally deranged character, was introduced in "Dagger Of The Mind." "The Corbomite Maneuver," is a story with a famous twist at the end, as an alien turns out to be young Clint Howard (most recently seen playing a scientist on the sci-fi series SPACE RANGERS). But the next two broadcasts consisted of "The Menagerie," which incorporated much of the footage from the first STAR TREK pilot, "The Cage."

"The Cage" had been filmed with a cast drawn from the original format, although the captain's name had been changed from Robert April to Christopher Pike. Pike was portrayed by Jeffrey Hunter, who had the rare distinction of having once played Jesus Christ, in KING OF KINGS. Leonard Nimoy appeared as Spock, but the character was a bit different from its later developments, as the logical aspect of his future personality belonged to the character Number One, portrayed by Majel Barrett.

"The Menagerie," as recounted in flashbacks by Spock, revealed a nascent version of the Enterprise crew as it is headed towards a Starbase after a disastrous first contact with an alien culture. In the story, Pike and crew were tired and in need of rest, but were distracted by a distress signal from a nearby planet.

When they investigated, they discovered a colony of scientists who had survived a crash, nearly twenty years earlier. . . and a beautiful young girl, Vina (Susan Oliver), who the survivors claimed was born just as their ship crashed. Something seemed odd, and when she lured Captain Pike away from the encampment, he was abducted by dome-skulled aliens and taken below the surface. The scientists and their camp, merely an illusion designed to lure humans, disappeared. This, told in flashbacks, ends ultimately with Pike's escape— but now he wishes to return to live out his life in a happy illusion, a quest which forms the framing device of Spock explaining his reasons for taking over the Enterprise.

"Balance of Terror" introduced the Romulans and marked the first appearance of Mark Lenard in the series. It also featured a bigoted crewman, an aspect Roddenberry would violently object to years later in STAR TREK VI as being out of sync with his view of the future of humanity in the 23rd century.

FROM THE DEAD

"Shore Leave," written by Theodore Sturgeon, marked the first time a leading STAR TREK character dies, only to return intact. (This time around it was McCoy.) It also has one of the longest fight scenes (between Kirk and Finnegan) in the history of series television.

"Tomorrow Is Yesterday" was the first solid time-travel story for STAR TREK, in which the Enterprise was hurled back to the 20th Century by the gravitational field of a black hole. "Space Seed" introduced Ricardo Montalban as Khan, a late-twentieth-century fanatic who, with his followers, has been adrift in a "sleeper ship' for hundreds of years.

"This Side of Paradise" took the Enterprise to a colony that should have died of radiation poisoning years earlier, but survived because of spores that also provided a constant sense of euphoria. The crew all fell prey to this, rendering them all unfit for (and uninterested in) their duties. Spock once again had his emotions liberated and fell in love, briefly, with a young botanist, played by the late, lovely Jill Ireland. Spock is called a Vulcanian in this story, a bit of a glitch in retrospect!

A notable Trek creature, "The Devil In The Dark," was the Horta, a silicon based creature that has been killing miners in the underground colony of Janus IV. "Errand of Mercy" sent Kirk to the peaceful pastoral world of Organia, which was in danger of Klingon attack; Klingon/Federation relations had become increasingly strained, and war seemed imminent. The Organians were in fact completely evolved beings whose human forms were a disguise, and, after defusing the conflict, they

> *STAR TREK is the most popular science fiction concept to ever appear on television, fathering two more series and a series of movies.*

promised to keep a watchful eye on the enemy factions.

"The Alternative Factor" involved the battle between Lazarus and his anti-matter double Lazarus; the fate of the universe hangs in the balance, and once again hinges on the need for dilithium crystals.

ONE OF THE BEST

"The City on the Edge of Forever" is regarded as one of the best STAR TREK episodes. Harlan Ellison's original script was rewritten by Gene Roddenberry which has become a long-standing source of annoyance for Ellison. Ellison's original version won the Writer's Guild of America award for screenwriting excellence.

"Operation: Annihilate" featured William Shatner in a second role: that of the dead body of Kirk's older brother George, complete with a mustache and gray hair. This personal tragedy was discovered on the planet Deneva, where alien parasites were attacking humans and driving them to their deaths with excruciating pain. This episode's effectiveness was somewhat underscored by the fact that the creatures look like enormous airborne fried eggs. Held to a wall with electromagnets, these creatures fell to the ground when hit by phaser fire.

The second season of STAR TREK began with "Amok Time," which also marked the first time DeForest Kelley received billing in the opening credits of the show. The story involves the Vulcan officer acting decidedly strange and sulky. McCoy determined that Spock will die if something is not done about the physical changes

he's undergoing. Spock told Kirk that he was undergoing pon farr, the Vulcan mating cycle, which would be fatal if he doesn't get to Vulcan and undergo the proper rituals posthaste.

Kirk bucked orders and rerouted the Enterprise to Vulcan, only to die, which had to come as a bit of a surprise for viewers. When the series was being rerun in the seventies, I heard of a case where a new fan watching this episode for the first time panicked when Kirk was declared dead.

The cast of STAR TREK was altered to include a new character in the second season, as well. The network was pressing for a character to rope in the "youth" market, something along the lines of Davey Jones of THE MONKEES. A press release (later revealed to have fabricated the incident) claimed that the show was criticized by the Russian Communist newspaper Pravda for, among other things, its lack of a Russian character in the Enterprise's otherwise multinational crew. To kill two birds with one stone, Roddenberry supposedly created the character of Ensign Pavel Chekov, a young officer with a heavy accent, to satisfy Soviet angst. Signing on as Chekov was actor Walter Koenig. Initially Koenig wore a wig until his hair grew long enough to match the look they wanted for him to have.

DEAD AGAIN

"The Changeling" was Nomad, an ancient Earth probe which had merged with an alien device and was convinced that its mission was to destroy imperfect life forms. Unfortunately, humans fit its criteria perfectly. Fortunately, it thought that Captain Kirk was the scientist Roykirk, the scientist who created it. Thus, it repaired Scotty after killing him (second Trek resurrection) out of deference to Kirk. It was still a threat, but Kirk managed to trick it into destroying itself. (In retrospect, this seems to have been one of his specialties.)

"Mirror, Mirror" cast Kirk, McCoy, Scotty and Uhura into an alternative universe where the Federation developed along bloodthirsty, Klingonesque lines. Written by Jerome Bixby, this remains one of the ten best episodes of Trek Classics.

"The Apple" was the gift Kirk brought to the peaceful, Eloi-like inhabitants of a dangerous world where their existence was protected by an ancient computer which also had retarded their social development. The Prime Directive notwithstanding, Kirk completely destroyed their social order and saved the Enterprise as well.

In "The Doomsday Machine," Commodore Matthew Decker, the sole survivor of the crew of the U.S.S. Constitution, took over the Enterprise in order to avenge himself of the device that wiped out his ship. (The basic idea would be reworked in "The Immunity Syndrome," but with a giant space amoeba!) This episode featured extensive use of special effects, including an AMT model Enterprise with the decal numbers switched around to stand in as a different starship.

"Catspaw" involved the efforts of two shape changing aliens to frighten the Enterprise crew with all the accoutrements of human superstition: magic, skeletons, witches and the like. Written by Robert Bloch, it was the Halloween episode of the second season.

MEET THE FOLKS

"Journey to Babel" finally introduced Spock's parents, the Vulcan Sarek (Mark Lenard) and his human wife Amanda (Jane Wyatt). While Mark Lenard plays the stoic Vulcan, this does establish his character in the series. Although not seen on the TV series again, Lenard has appeared in three of the STAR TREK motion pictures and two episodes of NEXT GENERATION as Sarek.

"The Deadly Years" afflicted Kirk and his main officers with a deadly disease causing accelerated aging. Shatner showed the least physical changes in the episode due to the actor's dislike of wearing a lot of special makeup.

"The Trouble With Tribbles" was a comical episode in which Klingons and furry little creatures that reproduce at an alarming rate threatened the peace on the Enterprise and an important grain shipment. Fortunately, the tribbles that ate the grain revealed that it was poisoned by a Klingon spy, and all ends well, with the Klingons getting stuck with the remaining tribbles.

"A Piece of the Action" was another humorous episode in which Kirk discovers a civilization that has modeled itself on the society described in a book left by a Federation mission one hundred years before. David Gerrold pitched an idea during the first season of THE NEXT GENERATION which would have been a sequel to this episode in which Picard and company visit this planet to discover

63

An underlying concept of STAR TREK was the Prime Directive, honored as much in its breach as in its observance.

that now the culture is patterned after Captain Kirk, Spock and everything involving the original starship Enterprise, but Roddenberry didn't go for the idea.

"A Private Little War" took place on the planet Neural, where Klingons were providing arms to escalate a tribal conflict preparatory to their own invasion. Kirk sought someone he knew on his last visit to this world, the leader Tyree, but was attacked by a vicious Mugatu, a horned yeti-like being, and became deathly ill from its poison.

TAMPERED CIVILIZATIONS

"Return to Tomorrow" found Kirk, Spock and Dr. Anne Mulhall lending their bodies to the disembodied minds of Sargon, Henoch and Thalassa, respectively, who were the sole survivors of their advanced civilization. "Patterns of Force" featured another civilization tampered with by a Federation emissary. In this case it was historian John Gill, who had tried to create an ordered society by using the structure of Nazi Germany.

This scheme had unfortunately backfired, and Gill was drugged and used as a figurehead by Melakon, a very unpleasant fellow. Gill's former history student James Kirk and Spock investigated, were captured, escaped and saved yet another addlebrained culture from itself. This was one of several STAR TREK episodes wherein the Enterprise visits a planet whose culture is patterned after a period of Earth's history.

"By Any Other Name" ultimately concerned alien spies who assumed human form only to be confounded by their own newfound

human nature. James Doohan has an amusing scene in which he gets an alien drunk.

"Omega Glory" featured yet another parallel history: the warring Kohms and Yangs paralleled the Communists and Yankees of the Vietnam War era. A starship captain had set himself as warlord with the Kohms; Kirk and Spock finally rallied the Yangs when Kirk realized that their sacred words were actually a distortion of the Preamble to the U.S. Constitution! All in all, one of the more heavy-handed episodes of STAR TREK, and it was written by Gene Roddenberry to boot! Roddenberry submitted this script to NBC to consider as a possible STAR TREK pilot script.

"The Ultimate Computer" was installed on the Enterprise, took command and decimated the crew of another starship when it mistakenly interpreted some Federation wargames as an actual attack. This features Captain Kirk once again displaying his uncanny ability to talk a computer to death.

WHEN IN ROME. . .

"Bread and Circuses" took Kirk and crew to a world with a history parallel to that of Earth, with one exception: this world's equivalent of the Roman Empire had lasted well into the 20th century. (This was undoubtedly very convenient as far as the wardrobe department was concerned.) The story also has a subplot involving a Christianity parallel which is used to provide a twist ending. It's still a weak episode in spite of that.

"Assignment Earth" incorporated the script of a pilot proposed by Roddenberry into the

STAR TREK continuity. Once again, the Enterprise crew travelled back into the past, this time to 1968. Here they met Gary Seven (Robert Lansing), a human (supposedly) trained by aliens to defend Earth. Kirk and Spock followed him to New York. Seven's mission was to prevent the launching of a Star-Wars type orbiting defense system that will actually prove disastrous to humanity.

With the help of Roberta Lincoln (Teri Garr) he managed to evade Kirk, but the captain eventually catches up with; Seven then managed to convince the captain of the importance of his mission, and the space bomb is destroyed. The story ended with a hint that Seven and Roberta would have more adventures, but a spin-off series never materialized.

The third season of STAR TREK began with a tale rightfully regarded as one of the worst Treks ever. In "Spock's Brain," the object in question is stolen. Don't worry, they get it back. In a bit of logic never explained, when Spock's brain is installed inside a computer, the voice of the computer is Nimoy's even though Spock's body was left behind on the Enterprise when his brain was stolen.

SPIES LIKE US

"The Enterprise Incident" sends the Enterprise on what is essentially an espionage mission: Kirk feigns a mental breakdown and takes the ship into the Neutral Zone. Outgunned by Romulans, he is captured, and Spock denounces his actions. McCoy beams to the Romulan ship just as Kirk attacks Spock; Spock kills Kirk with the Vulcan Death Grip and the body is beamed back to the Enterprise.

Of course, there is no Vulcan Death grip, and Kirk is revived, surgically altered to look like a Romulan, and beamed back to steal the Romulan cloaking device, the real object of this mission, while Spock diverts the attention of the Romulan commander, an attractive woman with a keen interest in the Vulcan. The Enterprise makes good its escape once Scotty gets the stolen cloaking device installed and working.

This cloaking device never made another appearance in the series, apparently because no one was interested in maintaining the continuity. We never do quite learn how Scotty can take a piece of Romulan technology and adapt it to working order in the Enterprise. Ever try making two completely incompatible computer systems work together when the other one is completely unknown to you?

"Is There In Truth No Beauty?" is the question posed when a Medusan comes on board; this race cannot be looked upon by humanoid eyes. Kolos, who stays in a protective case, is accompanied by the telepathic Dr. Miranda Jones. Marvick, an engineer on board, has been in love with Jones for years, and is driven by jealousy to try to kill Kolos. The sight of the alien drives him mad, and he goes, crazed, to engineering and casts the ship into strange uncharted regions of space.

The Medusan's amazing navigational powers are the only hope; Spock performs a mind meld wearing protective eyeglasses, but forgets them and is driven mad, too, after the ship is saved. Jones, who is revealed to be blind, must overcome her own jealous attachment to Kolos in order to help Spock. This episode features a spectacular special effects scene of the Enterprise at the edge of the galaxy.

DIMENSIONLESS

In "The Tholian Web," Kirk is stranded on a ship which is drifting between dimensions. His air supply is limited, and rescue efforts are hindered by the fact that the area of space causes humans to act aggressively towards each other. The Tholians, an unknown race, show up, accuse the Federation of trespassing, and begin to spin the web of the title. Spock eludes them, and Kirk is rescued just in the nick of time. Since Shatner is missing for act two and three, one wonders how he tolerated Nimoy having more lines than him in this episode, as Shatner was a notorious line-counter in scripts.

"Wink of an Eye" describes the condition of the Scalosians, whose radioactive water has sped up their life-rate so fast that they can only be perceived as a buzzing noise. When Kirk takes some of this water, he can perceive them, but his crew cannot sense him. The Scalosians plan to use him to repopulate their world. McCoy devise an antidote but Spock must first take some water and be sped up himself in order to find and save the Captain. This episode has the scene in which we see Kirk with the lovely girl and he's pulling his boot on in his bedroom.

"The Empath" is Gem, a beautiful mute woman. Kirk and McCoy are kidnapped and tortured by aliens; Gem is an empath who can absorb their pain and injuries, healing the terrible agonies inflicted on them. McCoy's injuries threaten to kill him, but she prevents this, risking her own life. This cruel test turns out to have a humane motivation, of sorts: two planets are threatened by an imminent disaster, but the aliens can only save the inhabitants of one, and have been trying to determine which race is more worthy of survival. Patterned in style after THE OUTER LIMITS episode "Nightmare," the story is largely filmed on simple sets unlit in the background so that the actors are constantly surrounded by blackness. It is effective for the mood of the story.

"Elaan of Troyius" is on the Enterprise heading to a diplomatically advantageous marriage, but she's more interested in Kirk; when she cries, the touch of her tears chemically induce Kirk to fall in love with her. Klingons confound matters, but all works out when Elaan's jewels turn out to be dilithium crystals. Kirk ultimately breaks free of her spell and she proceeds with her important mission. A simple-minded riff on Shakespeare's "The Taming Of The Shrew," the show uses Kirk's obsession with the Enterprise as the reason he's able to break the psycho-chemical spell the dolman is able to inflict with her tears.

MAKING LIGHT

"Let That Be Your Last Battlefield" tackles prejudice by reducing it to absurdity. Lokai, late of the planet Cheron, is half black and half white, being neatly bisected, pigmentwise, right down the middle. When he shows up on the

Enterprise, he is pursued by Bele, who looks exactly the same, except that his coloration makes him a mirror image of Lokai. When the Enterprise finally reaches Cheron, after nearly being demolished by the battles between the two passengers, it is revealed to be completely dead. Lokai and Cheron beam down to their world to continue their ancient, pointless conflict to their deaths. Late in the episode it ran short so we're treated to seeing Bele and Lokai running down corridor after corridor after corridor until they finally reach the Transporter room.

"Requiem for Methuselah" takes Kirk and crew to Holberg 917-G in search of the antidote to a deadly disease. There they encounter a Mr. Flint and Reena, a beautiful young lady, and Kirk falls for her right off the bat. Eventually it is discovered that Flint is actually an immortal who lived on Earth for centuries; among his aliases were Da Vinci and Brahms. Without Earth's atmosphere to preserve him, his immortality is nearing its end. Reena is the last of a series of androids he has constructed to keep him company. This bothers Kirk more than a bit, so Spock obligingly clears Kirk's mind of the unhappy memory. That last scene where Spock says "Forget" is particularly touching as this was the last episode rerun on NBC in August 1969 when the show was cancelled.

"The Way To Eden" is sought by the charismatic but crazed Dr. Sevrin and his youthful disciples, who could only be described as space hippies. Walter Koenig, who played the youth-oriented Chekov, was forced to act like a pro-establishment stiff when he meets the Hippies. In "The Savage Curtain" the Enterprise is hailed by Abraham Lincoln, who just happens to be floating in space nearby. It could happen!

"All Our Yesterdays" involves another time portal through which Kirk, Spock and McCoy pass. This one is located on the planet Sarpeidon, whose people have fled an impending nova by relocating to various different periods in their past history. Kirk goes through first and winds up in an era similar to Reformation England, where he is in danger of being killed as a witch. Spock and the doctor find themselves in a prehistoric ice age, where the Vulcan reverts to his ancestors' lustful ways and becomes involved with a woman, Zarabeth.

They believe that they cannot return to their temporal starting point without dying, but this is not actually true as they did not undergo the necessary treatments. Meanwhile, Kirk resolves his troubles with the help of another time traveller, and manages to reclaim his friends and get back to the ship just before the nova destroys the planet. The episode ends with a nice special effect shot of the Enterprise leaving a solar system while a star goes nova in the background.

A PLACE IN HISTORY

"Turnabout Intruder," the final STAR TREK episode to be filmed, was dubbed "Captain Kirk, Space Queen" by the crew. Here, a woman once spurned by Kirk in favor of his Starfleet career gets her revenge by switching bodies with him and and taking over his ship! Spock determines the truth of this

67

by using a Vulcan mind meld on Dr. Janice Lester's body, where he finds the mind of Kirk, but has a hard time convincing anyone that Kirk's body is occupied by a woman. Eventually, McCoy is brought in on this, only to be accused of mutiny along with Spock, and sentenced to death. By this point, everyone realizes that something is drastically amiss, and Kirk shakes off the effects of the mind transfer. This is a strange episode as Janice Lester is portrayed as a woman who hates being female and is jealous of Kirk largely because he's a man.

With this, the series ended its initial network run (summer reruns notwithstanding) and seemed fated for oblivion. It had already been the focus of two letter campaigns: the first, organized by Harlan Ellison, had been signed by noted science fiction authors in an attempt to get good science fiction writing on the air; despite Ellison's contribution and the presence of such writers as Robert Bloch and Theodore Sturgeon on the show, Ellison, for one, felt that the show failed to live up to its potential. The second letter campaign was organized by fan Bjo Trimble and is generally given credit for saving the series during its second season; it could also thus be deemed responsible for the third season and such clunkers as "Spocks Brain."

But nothing would save STAR TREK now— except syndication. And of course, that is history.

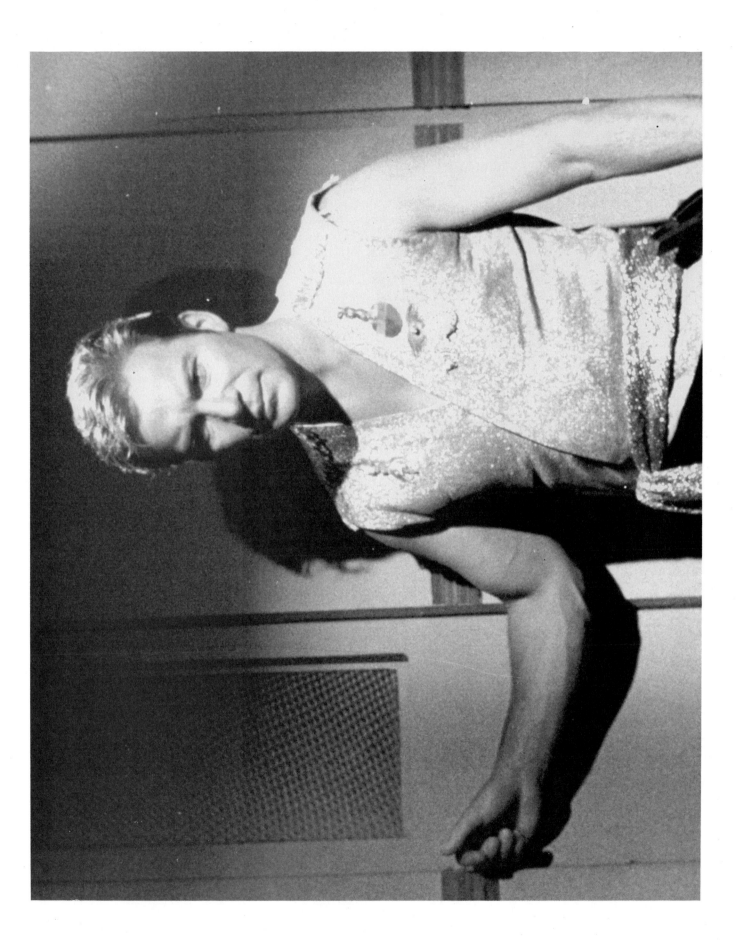

Pigeon-holed as an afternoon soap opera, this series dis-

pensed with adultery and pregnancy and instead explored all the

classic elements of the horror genre!

To this day it is remembered. Even the sound of its haunting theme music used as the background for cheapo late night commercials for a telephone "reincarnationist" (call this 976 number, and for four bucks a minute you can find out who you were in a previous life!) brings back memories. Memories of waves crashing on a barren New England shore in slow motion while a dark, Gothic mansion looms high atop the cliffs above. Memories of vampires and werewolves, witches and time travel.

It all began on June 27, 1966— sort of. This marked the debut of producer Dan Curtis' daily soap opera DARK SHADOWS. Those few viewers who were on hand that day witnessed the fairly unremarkable tale of a young woman named Victoria Winters, and her arrival at the seaside town of Collinsport, a decaying Colonial-era location where she was to begin her duties as the governess to a young boy named David Collins. The head of the Collins family was one Elizabeth Collins, played by one-time Hollywood star Joan Bennett. Victoria found herself a character in a low-budget black-and-white Gothic soap which drifted dangerously close to cancellation during the course of its first year on screen. The budget was actually so low that the writers were only allowed to use a maximum of five characters in any single episode!

Curtis noticed, however, that ratings picked up during a story sequence that involved a ghost in the Collins mansion. Inspired by this, in June 1967 he introduced another character, Barnabas Collins, a relative who arrives in Collinsport and claims to be from England. Strange events, involving dead animals begin to occur, and eventually viewers discovered that the mannered, vaguely sinister Barnabas had not come from England at all, but had been in Collinsport for the previous two hundred years until Willie Loomis freed him from his coffin! Yes, Barnabas was actually a vampire! If Barnabas had never been written into the series, it is almost a one hundred per cent certainty that DARK SHADOWS would be barely remembered today.

A plot device which was born of desperation, was in fact destined to keep DARK SHADOWS going for another four years, and would give birth to one of the most dedicated fan followings of any television series. In fact, when the supernatural angle began to deepen, the audience doubled. A large part of this audience was rather young— what kid could resist a show with vampires and witches that was on television every day, and just about the time school let out?

GOTHIC SOAP

DARK SHADOWS

A TRUE EPIC

DARK SHADOWS was a true television epic! Just scanning a brief resume of the series shows that it covered a lot of ground. After his introduction, the secret of Barnabas Collins was unveiled. Soon other characters came to know of his curse, and it became readily apparent that he was an unwilling monster (note his tendency early in the show to use only animals to fulfill his sanguinary thirst) with a bit of a tragic streak. Soon enough, Baranabas had a human ally, albeit one often at odds with him: Dr. Julia Hoffman, who strove to help him overcome his vampirism. Things really picked up steam when a séance was held in the mansion of Collinswood and one of the participants disappeared. This was the long-suffering Victoria, who returned to her senses to find herself still in Collinsport—in 1795! This two-month sequence really boosted the ratings for DARK SHADOWS and saved the show from oblivion.

Now that Barnabas had become the hero of the series, a new villain would soon be introduced. Victoria, trapped in the past, can't help but notice that everyone looks a lot like people she knew in the Twentieth Century. In the case of Barnabas, of course, this is because he is the same person she knew, but in the case of the others, it was because the show's budget (remember that five-person-per-episode limit?) made it desirable, if not in fact necessary, to have the same actors play the ancestors of their modern characters. But there was one character not recognized: Angelique, the maid of the DuPres family.

Victoria's Eighteenth Century tribulations included being put on trial as a witch. But the real witch was actually Angelique, who was in love with Barnabas and determined to keep him forever apart from his true love, Josette. It was Angelique's jealousy and anger at rejection which led her to put a curse on Barnabas and turn him into a vampire. He, in turn, is not as nice a fellow in his first days as a vampire as he would be after a couple of centuries of coffin-bound contemplation, and he sets out to win Josette eternally by the time-honored vampire technique. However, his nocturnal prowlings are stoped by his own father, Joshua Collins, when he realizes what has befallen his son. Barnabas is put in the coffin where he will sleep until—well, until 1967. Victoria's own difficulties bring her to the brink of execution but she is whisked back to modern times just at the last moment.

Things only picked up their pace from here on out. Reincarnation, warlocks, aliens, curses, and countless other supernatural and science fiction oddities all had their day, with Barnabas at the center of the maelstrom. Another time travel plot carried characters back to 1897, as well. By the end of 1968, a new character with a problem was on hand: Quentin Collins, whose own curse was more lycanthropic in nature. (With a werewolf on hand, Barnabas was able to get some much needed rest from time to time).

ALL GOOD THINGS MUST COME TO AN END

Like all good things, DARK SHADOWS had to come to an end, and its final episode was aired on April 2, 1971, leaving its labrynthine plotlines tangled and unfinished. The storyline underway at the end of the series was yet another time travel sequence, this time back to 1840. It was amazing how the show captured so many imaginations. After all, it was a one shot deal back then and this was a low budget show with a lot of mistakes.

One of DARK SHADOWS' most famous foul-ups occurred in a scene where Jonathan Frid (as Barnabas) was throttling Grayson Hall (as Dr. Julia Hoffman). Frid's line was a simple one: "I'm going to kill you!" But, as will sometimes happen to thespians, he managed to forget it. Finally, his victim gathered her wits and gasped, in character, "You're not going to kill me, are you?" To which Frid quickly responded: "Oh, yes. . . I'm going to kill you!"

Producer Dan Curtis was determined to make the most of the show's concept. Even before the demise of the DARK SHADOWS series, he took his creation to MGM and was given a 1 million dollar budget for directing his first feature, HOUSE OF DARK SHADOWS. This was essentially a retelling of the early Barnabas plotline, with the notable difference that most of the characters in this version die.

A second feature, NIGHT OF DARK SHADOWS, went before the cameras without Barnabas Collins (Jonathan Frid had decided, after nearly five years of the character, to hang up his teeth). So NIGHT OF DARK SHADOWS, of necessity, became the tale of werewolf Quentin Collins' conflict with the witch Angelique. MGM did well enough with this outing that the studio wanted yet another DARK SHADOWS feature. By this time, Curtis and his accomplices were pretty tired of Collinsport themselves, and declined the offer.

The cast of the original DARK SHADOWS was an interesting one. Jonathan Frid, the original Barnabas Collins, was a Shakespearean actor who originally

DARK SHADOWS was something new on television. Nothing like it had ever been seen before, or would be after its disappearance.

signed on for a few week's work only to be forever linked with the character, much as Leonard Nimoy could never shake Spock. (Although when Frid said that he quit, it stuck.) Quentin the werewolf was played by David Selby, who later came to fame on the prime-time soap opera FALCON CREST as the character of Richard Channing.

Victoria Winters was played by Alexandra Moltke, at the time a top model, whose acting career was largely forgotten by all but DARK SHADOWS afficionadoes until she achieved a different sort of notoriety years later as a witness in the famous Claus Von Bulow case. Various unknowns who appeared on DARK SHADOWS only to achieve fame elsewhere later

73

included Kate Jackson (Daphne) of CHARLIE'S ANGELS and THE SCARECROW AND MRS. KING fame, Marsha Mason, and future Broadway ("A Chorus Line") star Donna McKechnie.

THE AFTER LIFE

After DARK SHADOWS, producer/creator Dan Curtis went on to create the TV-movie THE NIGHT STALKER, a superb Richard Matheson script about a second-string newspaper reporter (Darren McGavin) in Las Vegas who discovers that a serial killer is actually a vampire. This spawned another TV movie and a full fledged, if short lived, series in which the reporter Kolchak encountered various supernatural creatures on a weekly basis.

Curtis later achieved great success as the man behind the two blockbuster miniseries THE WINDS OF WAR and WAR AND REMEMBRANCE, which were based on Herman Wouk's novels about World War Two. Through all this, Curtis was often sent inquiries from various networks about reviving DARK SHADOWS, but generally demurred. The time wasn't right.

In 1991, the time finally came. NBC announced that DARK SHADOWS would be returning to television in prime time with an all-new cast! The first five hours would be directed by Curtis. As Barnabas Collins, the new DARK SHADOWS starred British actor Ben Cross, who had achieved fame a decade or so earlier as one of the stars of the Oscar-winning feature CHARIOTS OF FIRE. The role of Elizabeth Collins Stoddard was taken this time by actress Jean

Simmons, who had an illustrious, decades-long career in film behind her (THE ROBE, THE BIG COUNTRY and many other classics of the fifties and Sixties) as well as an equally impressive resumé of television work including a recent dramatic guest appearance on STAR TREK—THE NEXT GENERATION as a paranoid admiral who tries to bring down Captain Jean-Luc Picard.

Roger Collins was portrayed by veteran television actor Roy Thinnes, best known perhaps for his part in the science fiction series THE INVADERS. The crucial role of Victoria Winters was assumed by Joanna Going, an alumnus of the daily soap opera Another World. The tough-as-nails Doctor Julia Hoffman was played by horror flick veteran Barbara Steele (THE PIT AND THE PENDULUM).

POOR WILLIE

As Willie, the all-important discoverer of Barnabas' resting place, the show cast Jim Fyfe, who gave this dim fellow a certain creepy charm. Fyfe himself described Willie as being like Newhart's Larry, Darryl and Darryl "gone very, very wrong." And considering the possibility that Willie might become a vampire, Fyfe mused that "it would be good if being a vampire could get Willie some babes." Alas for poor Willie, all he ever got during the series was a taste of how thankless it was to be employed as the chief flunky to a very moody vampire who obviously got extremely stressed out by being so darn nice to just about everybody else. Being Barnabas' Renfield-in-waiting was no picnic.

Perhaps if the show had run longer, Willie might have gotten such job benefits as immortality and blood hunger, but time was too much short for the DARK SHADOWS revival.

But what a revival it was! Two decades earlier, DARK SHADOWS was perhaps the lowest budgeted series on television, with its notorious production problems and constant snafus. But DARK SHADOWS, 90's-style, was a lush, full bodied revival in every sense of the word; as a vampire is revived by a good quenching draft of human hemoglobin, so, too, was the show revitalized by the twenty or so million dollars which NBC sunk into its throat— er, budget.

The opening recreates the basic DARK SHADOWS introduction, replete with a new arrangement of the show's original theme. As so often in the past, the opening is narrated as if from Victoria's diary, as waves crash once more on the rocks beneath the cliffs surmounted by Collinswood. (Collinswood, like every other aspect of the new DARK SHADOWS, was "portrayed" by a different "actor," in this case a mansion on the California coast.)

Like the first DARK SHADOWS movie, this is basically a remake of the original series. Victoria comes to work for the Collins family and meets its various members, all of whom have various soap-opera style secrets— including the just-arrived British Collins, Barnabas (the remake of course dispenses with the first Barnabas-less year or it would have been slow going for sure), whose personal secret is the biggest secret of them all.

INTERESTING TOUCHES

In the original DARK SHADOWS it was the modern-day Maggie who reminded the resurrected Barnabas Collins of his long-lost love Josette, in the new DARK SHADOWS it was Victoria Winters herself who filled this role. The cast did a fine job recreating the characters on the luxurious new Collinsport sets and locations, some veering more into the edges of hamming it up perhaps, but with Ben Cross being suitably icy and reserved with sudden dark flashes of tormented, blood-churning passion.

As with the original series, things really started rolling when a seance was held in Collinswood and Victoria was again transported back to the Eighteenth Century to witness the tragic drama leading up to the vampirization of Barnabas Collins. As before, the same actors portrayed their modern characters and their ancestors, while Joanna Going as Victoria actually had to cope with seeing Josette, also played by Going.

This sequence, which ran concurrently with modern-day sequences, had some interesting touches. (One would assume that this meant that there was a certain parallelism going between the two eras as far as duration of action was concerned.) One nice touch: Victoria's displacement was balanced by the removal of an Eighteenth Century woman to modern times— a woman who was on her way to Collinsport to act as a nanny! This character basically freaked out and spent most of her

DARK SHADOWS

time under sedation, waking up occasionally to freak out again.

Another amusing touch was the bewilderment of the Eighteenth Century characters at Victoria's clothes—especially at the washing instruction symbols on the tag of her dress! This of course would really lead to trouble as these would eventually be seen as cabalistic symbols of evil when Victoria was accused of witchcraft by the hypocritical Reverend Trask, played with scenery-chewing relish by Roy Thinnes.

Of course, there was real witchery about in the person of Angelique, who, after turning her ex-lover into a vampire, certainly wasn't above framing someone else for her own misdeeds. And as before, Victoria came perilously close to being executed, only to be whisked back to her own time in the end, returning the other woman back to her own in the process. But what of Angelique? Suffice it to say, Lysette Anthony was perfect in the part, a truly gorgeous woman who brought just the roght tone of conniving— er, witchiness to the role.

THE RATINGS DON'T LIE

Despite the high quality of the production overall, the ratings were not kind to the new DARK SHADOWS in the end. True, the pilot episodes drew good ratings but then attention dropped off as the series proper went on, and Victoria returned to the Twentieth Century just in time for the Nielsen axe to fall. No time for Quentin, the resurgence of Angelique or any of the other DARK SHADOWS plotlines that would have made for great viewing in the new version.

And, sadly, Ben Cross' own comments after the show was cancelled leave little doubt that he would not be on hand for any future revival. But then, how many lives can one television series have? At least the original DARK SHADOWS is now pretty much available on video, the only daily television series ever to be so available commercially.

And so, for true DARK SHADOWS lovers everywhere, the test of loyalty is only limited by the size of their savings accounts!

76

THE PRISONER demonstrated that an on-going series could tell unusual stories which were entertaining and captivating. Number Six demonstrated that the only prisoners were those in the audience who had been held captive by the narrow possibilities presented in typical prime time fare.

Born in New York on March 19, 1928 (also the birthdate given by Number Six!) and raised in Ireland, Patrick McGoohan was already a star in Great Britain and known in America by the time THE PRISONER made its television debut. McGoohan had achieved this prominence as the star of DANGER MAN (known in the United States as SECRET AGENT), which had premiered in Britain in September 1960, thus actually predating the screen appearance of James Bond! In the fifty-four episodes of SECRET AGENT, McGoohan had played John Drake, an operative in the employ of N.A.T.O. Unlike Bond, Drake (largely at McGoohan's insistence) was not cavalier in his attitude towards women, violence or his job.

A real gentleman, Drake did not do in his foes in the thrill of victory. He was a real professional, and one who believed in fair play. Drake also had his share of high-tech gadgetry and pretty women. However, Drake kept his professional cool and, unlike Bond, did not take advantage of any woman who took a fancy to him, perhaps breaking as many hearts as Bond but doing it like a real gentleman, and for truly gentlemanly reasons.

After a run as a half-hour show in 1960 and 1961, SECRET AGENT went off the air only to return as an hour-long series in 1965 and 1966. (It was the hour version which achieved a good bit of success across the pond in the U.S.A.) But McGoohan soon became tired of the limited creative possibilities of doing a spy series, which was, by this time, only one among countless post-Bond espionage tales in practically every medium. Fortunately, he had enough star power that he was given free reign by Lew Grade, and he developed THE PRISONER, which premiered in Britain in 1967 (and which made obscure ripples in a late summertime replacement slot on CBS in 1968).

THE PRISONER series began, appropriately enough, with "Arrival." In a quick montage, the world (and public image) of a man who seems to be John Drake is turned quickly upside down. For unknown reasons, an angry McGoohan storms into the secret headquarters of some London-based organization, resigns, and drives, grim-faced, back to his home and begins to pack for a journey. His travel plans are interrupted when a gas is pumped into his apartment, rendering him unconscious, and when he awakes it is to find himself in The Village. A strange place, with oddly cheerful people, it is located, on a map the as-yet unnamed McGoohan character obtains, simply between the mountains and the sea— which are called just that, "The Mountains" and "The Sea," on the utterly useless map!

NUMBER SIX
MEETS NUMBER TWO

Given an apartment, he receives a call on his phone (numbered 'six') and is invited out to breakfast, where he meets first The Butler and then Number Two (Guy Doleman). He learns that someone wants to know all the things he knows, beginning with the reason for his resignation. He resists Number Two's interrogation and also defies the number he has been assigned—although, oddly, Number Six never attempts to counter his numbering by ever using his real name!

Number Six discovers the eerie quality of the Village, with its seemingly-happy inhabitants, all of whom are prisoners like himself. (Most insidiously, canned muzak is played throughout the Village all day!) He witnesses Rover, the balloon-like watchdog device of the Village, fatally foil an attempted escape. Number Six begins to seek a way out himself, but encounters surveillance everywhere, and is hospitalized after a run-in with Rover. Here he meets another prisoner named Cobb, who involves him in an elaborate escape plan—which ultimately proves to be a set-up intended to demonstrate to Number Six the futility of trying to get away.

In "The Chimes of Big Ben" we encounter a different Number Two, portrayed this time around by Leo McKern (later known for his role as Rumpole of the Bailey.) Apparently there is a high turnover in the job. This Number Two, like his predecessor tries to discover Number Six's reason for resigning. This Number Two is a cheery, philosophical fel-low; the plot involves yet another escape attempt by Number Six which takes him all the way back to his London flat— or does it? Even his former superiors seem to be in on the deception, which just underscores the supposition that it was they who engineered his kidnapping.

In "A, B And C," Number Six is subjected to a dream control experiment. Yet another Number Two (Colin Gordon) has a pet theory that Number Six resigned because he was about to sell secrets, and has Number 14 use a drug of her own design, along with other techniques, to recreate in Number Six's mind a party he attended in Paris shortly before his resignation. Who— suspects A, B, or C— was he going to sell his important papers to? But even under sedation, Number Six's will subtly warps the course of these experiments— and by the time of his third session, he is on to what's happening and manages to stay conscious and really throw a wrench into the scenario. The "papers" turn out to have been travel pamphlets— whatever Number Six's reason for quitting, he was not selling out or defecting, but he did plan to take a decent vacation after his resignation.

DIABOLICAL PLOTS

"Free For All," written and directed by McGoohan, involves Number Six in a "democratic" election for the post of Number Two (Eric Portman, this time around). Of course this is all a sham; the skeptical Number Six reluctantly takes part. True, he actually "wins" the office of Number Two, only to discover, when he tells all the

Villagers that they are free, that they don't even realize that they are prisoners; the Village, to them, is an illusion of freedom.

"The Schizoid Man" faces Number Six with a truly diabolical scheme to break him. Number Twelve (twelve being the double of six) is altered to look exactly like Number Six. Then, Number Six is subjected to various reconditioning so that such aspects as his right-handedness and other habits are changed. He is then treated as if he is Number Twelve, a trusted Villager, and he is enlisted by Number Two (Anton Rodgers) to aid in the effort to break a most troublesome newcomer— Number Six!

The real Number Six's efforts to prove that he is the real Number Six are subverted by becoming part of the process by which the Village is pretending to attempt to break the false Number Six—the real item can't even assert his own identity without collaborating, on another level, with his enemies! Ultimately, he manages to turn the tables so that, once Rover kills the real Number Twelve (in other words, the false Number Six— confusing, isn't it?), Number Two thinks he's the other Six. A simple slip clues Number Two in, but he lets Number Six go, only to return him immediately, revealing to Number Six and the audience that there is still no escape.

In "The General," Number Six tries to stop an insidious speed learning process which is actually a mind control technique. Even the Professor who invented it has had second thoughts and tried to escape. Ultimately, The General of the title turns out to be the comput-er behind the whole thing, which Number Six manages to destroy through largely philosophical means.

BETRAYED AGAIN

In "Many Happy Returns," Number Six awakes to find the Village deserted and all its functions—water, power, et cetera—terminated. Unobserved (except by a cat) he fashions a boat and sails away, finally hitching a ride with some contentious gunrunners, and makes his way back to London, arriving the day before his birthday. Here, his former superiors (different from the ones portrayed in "The Chimes of Big Ben") agree, after much consideration of his story, to help him try to find the Village. He also finds his apartment occupied by a Mrs. Butterworth, who lends him the use of his own car and promises to bake him a cake for his birthday. Ultimately, Six is betrayed again, and he winds up back in the Village—but Mrs. Butterworth does keep her promise to him, and waltzes into his Village apartment with the cake.

"Dance of the Dead," originally second in the series but aired later in the run, finds the newly-arrived Number Six on trial for violating the rules of the Village— rules he and no one else in the Village have never been informed of. "Do Not Forsake Me Oh My Darling" takes Number Six back out of the Village. In London, former superiors (again different!) are wondering what happened to him when he vanished a year earlier; before he resigned he'd been on the trail of a Professor Seltzman, leaving only some seemingly innocuous holiday photos. Seltzman had been working on a mind-transfer machine. . . and back in the Village, Number Six has his mind switched into a Colonel's body with one of these devices and is sent to resume the quest for the Professor.

Back in London again, he must convince his former associates, and his fiancée, that he is who he says he is, as well as finding his quarry. He and Seltzman are ultimately taken back to the Village, where Seltzman sets matters aright, but actually pulls a three-way switch: Number Six gets his own body back, but the Colonel has his mind switched into Seltzman's body, a fact Number Two (Clifford Evans) realizes only after he's sent the "Colonel" away after a job well done!

As if to make up for the lack of a Number Two in "Many Happy Returns,'" the episode "It's Your Funeral" features two of them, a retiring Number Two, and his stand-in/heir apparent. Number Six, meanwhile, gets involved with the Jammers, rebellious Villagers who annoy their watchers by openly planning escapes and other radical acts but never actually committing them; the plots of known Jammers are thus ignored by the powers-that-be. Number Six discovers that some of them are actually planning to assassinate the old Number Two, and that the incoming Number Two is behind it; the scheme is yet another Village device, which will give an excuse to punish the Villagers, something Number Six swears to stop.

In "Checkmate" Number Six engineers a mass escape but fails when his co-conspirators come to believe that he is one of their jailers and that the plot is a test of their loyalty.

WILD WILD WEST

"Living In Harmony" dispenses with the usual episode opening; instead, it's told as a Western, with Number Six as a resigning sheriff who is abducted and taken to a town called Harmony. Number Two (David Bauer) appears as the town's Judge, with the Kid (Alexis Kanner), later revealed to be Number Eight, as his crazed enforcer. The usual efforts are given a twist: the sheriff has forsworn his guns, and the efforts to break him take the form of trying to force him to kill. Ultimately, Number Six overcomes this drug-induced situation, finds himself in a deserted Western set with cardboard cutout characters, and returns to the Village, where the failed drama spills over into reality.

When THE PRISONER was first shown in the United States in 1968, this episode was left out—although one was able to see if on a Canadian TV station at the time. It's unknown whether this was left out because there was one episode too many to run in the summer season, or because the network feared viewers would be confused by the fact that the episode lacked the familiar opening title sequence.

"A Change of Mind" finds Number Six ostracized by the Village for "unmutual" behavior. He is then tricked into thinking that he has undergone a behavior-altering brain operation, when he is actually only being drugged, a fact he eventually works out. Ultimately he turns the tables on this episode's Number Two (John Sharpe), who is himself declared "unmutual" and hounded out of the Village back into the control bunker.

"Hammer Into Anvil" features the nastiest Number Two on record (Patrick Cargill) as well as Number Six's most personal vendetta against anyone to hold that post. The catalyst is Number Seventy-Three, a woman who has attempted suicide to escape the Village. Having failed, she is interrogated by the cruel Number Two; the Village wants to know where her husband is, but she refuses, and jumps out of a hospital window to her death. Number Six witnesses this and sets out to destroy this Number Two; he begins to act as if he's involved in some sort of conspiracy.

His meaningless gestures are interpreted as such by Number Two, and the inability of Number Two's underlings to get to the bottom of this nonexistent plot leads him first to suspect them all of complicity, and ultimately into utter paranoia. Finally, he comes to believe that Number Six is a Village plant sent to test him; having failed, he begs Six to turn him in, but Six forces one final humiliation on him and forces Number Two to call Number One himself. Revenge for Number Seventy-Three is thus complete.

COMPLEX? TOO BAD

"The Girl Who Was Death" was Patrick McGoohan's slap at British viewers who complained about the complexity and obscurity of THE PRISONER and complained about wanting shows more reminiscent of the old John Drake days. It is a wild, funny and rather silly parody of spy action plots (with a nod, perhaps, to the sly attitude of THE AVENGERS) which does not turn out to be another drug-induced or dream scenario designed to break Number Six but is merely a story that he had been reading to a group of Village children (with Number Two and his assistant as the heavies). The tip-off comes at the end when Number Six looks into a surveillance camera and says "Goodnight, children. . . everywhere." Although he's talking

Rather than "power to the people", a popular slogan of the time, THE PRISONER advocated the power of the individual.

to Number Two, who hoped he'd drop his guard among children, he's also addressing those viewers whom he's just coddled by giving them a sly taste of the kind of show they were able to understand better than the usual symbol-laden Prisoner episode.

"Once Upon A Time" began the end of the series. Number Two (Leo McKern) is back and determined to break Number Six, and gets Number One to decree "absolute degree." The Village focuses all its powers on Number Six; everyone else is cleared out except Two, Six and The Butler. A detailed synopsis would take many pages but it all boils down to Two taking Six back through his life but finding him a tough nut to crack from childhood on up. Their one-on-one battle of wits grows truly intense; this Number Two, a genial fellow in his first appearance, becomes more and more frenzied. The deadline arrives with Number

Six unbroken, and Number Two drops dead.

Confounded enough by the previous episode, viewers found "Fall Out" hard to take. The dead Number Two is revived; Number Six is declared an individual but is obviously expected to cooperate on some other higher level, and he actually escapes— but to what? If you haven't seen this episode it would be unfair to detail all its riches in a synopsis, but if it baffled you when you saw it, perhaps Patrick McGoohan himself could shed some light on this episode and on the Prisoner series as a whole.

In 1977, Patrick McGoohan was interviewed on Canadian television and he spoke freely and candidly about the origins of THE PRISONER, what it all meant, what he intended and if sometimes more is read into a scene or idea than was initially intended. Never seen on American television, this was quite possibly the only lengthy and detailed interview ever done with him on this subject. Whereas he had been questioned about it in previous interviews, he had seemed reluctant to give away the show's "secrets," perhaps because it was much more recent then. At the time of the Canadian interview, nearly ten years had passed since the series aired and even Public Television Stations were airing episodes and afterwards pontificating on what it all meant.

HERE'S TO CONTROVERSY

THE PRISONER has become the most controversial series to appear on television just by the very virtue of the fact that it took advantage of the medium to stretch itself into corners and con- cepts never before explored on the living room screen. Using the time-honored literary staples of allusion, symbolism and allegory, it sought to comment on our structured and ordered society by creating an artificial setting which was even more structured and ordered. When it was first run in the U.S. in the summer of 1968, and then repeated a year later, it was greeted with amazement, and not a little disbelief. Some people honestly couldn't tell if it was fish or foul. Even a simple comment on the obvious social commentary of the phrase "I am not a number, I am a free man" could be greeted by the opinion that such a view was reading too much into what was really only a television show.

Time has shown it to be much more than that. Many myths have been built up around the show, including references to unproduced scripts and a longer series than merely seventeen episodes. But as Patrick McGoohan tells it, quite the opposite was true.

He had made 54 episodes of SECRET AGENT (which has also been run under the title DANGER MAN), and was tired with that and looking for something else to go on to. The financial backer of the series, Sir Lew Grade, was unhappy with McGoohan's wish to quit but finally asked him what he wanted to do instead.

"I had a whole format prepared," McGoohan explained," which initially came from one of the places on SECRET AGENT. It was a place called Portmeiron, where a great deal of it was shot, and I thought it was an extraordinary place architecturally and atmosphere-wise. I thought it should be used for something. That was two years before the concept came to me. So I prepared it and I went to see Lew Grade. I had photographs of the village, whatever, and a format, and he said, I don't want to read the format because he doesn't read formats.

IT'S ALWAYS ABOUT MONEY

"He said he doesn't read apart from accounts. And he sort of said, What's it about? tell me. So I talked for ten minutes and he stopped me and said, I don't understand one word you're talking about, but how much is it going to be? So I had a budget with me, oddly enough, and I told him how much and he said, When can you start? I said Monday on the script, and he said, the money will be in your company's account on Monday morning, and that's how we started."

Initially, McGoohan only wanted to do THE PRISONER as a mini-series of seven episodes. "I thought that the concept of the thing would sustain for only seven. But then Lew Grade wanted to make his sale to CBS, I believe, and he said he couldn't make a sale unless he had more, and he wanted twenty-six. I couldn't conceive of twenty-six stories because it would be spreading it very thin, but we did manage, over the weekend with my writers, to cook up ten more outlines. Eventually we did seventeen, but it should have been seven."

When McGoohan assembled the writers for the series, they were people who were accustomed to writing for THE SAINT and SECRET AGENT. They found this unusual new series somewhat difficult to adjust to. "We lost a few by the wayside," McGoohan said. "I sat down and I wrote a forty page sort of history of the village, from the telephones they used, what they ate, the sewage systems, the transport, the boundary, the description of the village, every aspect of it. They were all given copies of this and then, naturally, we talked to them about it and sent them away and hoped they'd come up with an idea that was feasible."

He explained to them that the Village was a place which wanted to destroy the individual, to break his spirit so that Number Six would accept his situation and live happily in the Village forever. But Number Six was the one rebel that they couldn't break. Into this was added McGoohan's own impatience with numerology in society, "and the way we're being made into ciphers, so there was something else beside it."

McGoohan revealed that besides the final two episodes which appeared with his name as screenwriter, that he also wrote others, those appearing under pseudonyms, such as "Free For All" by Paddy Fitz.

WHO'S LAUGHING LAST?

He's gratified by the mystique which has built up around the series because it received a rather mixed reception when it first appeared on the British airwaves. "There were a lot of haters of it. A love/hate relationship, whichever way you looked at it. Already there was a small cult, and now there is a much bigger one over there. In fact, when the last episode came out in England, it had one of the largest

85

Only eighteen episodes were ever aired, but THE PRISONER left a permanent mark in the history of television.

viewing audiences because everyone wanted to know who was Number One. When they finally saw it there was a near riot and I was going to be lynched. I had to go into hiding in the mountains for two weeks until things calmed down. It's true. They were angry because they hadn't found out who Number One was.

It went by quickly and they refused to acknowledge it. That was deliberate. I forget how many frames. I think there were fifty-two frames of the shot when they pulled off the monkey mask and then Number One's a monkey and then Number One's himself. It was deliberate. I mean, I could have held it there for a good two minutes and put a subtitle on it saying 'It's Him!' but I thought that I wasn't going to pander to a mentality so low that it couldn't perceive what I was trying to say. So you had to be a little quick to pick it up, that's all."

Regarding that initial response, McGoohan expressed delight. "I wanted to have controversy, arguments, fights, discussion and anger; waving of fists in my face saying, 'How dare you! Why don't you do more SECRET AGENT's so we can understand?' I was delighted with that reaction. I think it was a very good one. That was the intention of the exercise."

When questioned about the response from politicians, bureaucrats and the like, he said, "Not enough. They stood clear, but of course they'd be the very ones who wouldn't understand it."

He explained that "Living In Harmony" came about for a surprising reason, especially since it's one of the most interesting episodes. "I wanted to do a Western. I had never done one, and they'd never made a Western in England and they were short a story so we cooked that one up. We wrote it in four days and shot it and it was fun. So whatever concept you put into it, that's the reason for it. Then we sort of stepped the figures up a bit and put some other concepts which have other levels, sociological levels, which you can make what you want out of them."

ALL BY DESIGN

On the subject of circumstances resulting in the creation of something which later appeared to be deep inspiration, he talked about Rover. "Rover, yes. Now, the reason that happened. . . . again, it's like the Western. We had this marvelous piece of machinery built which was going to be Rover, and this thing was like a hover craft and it would go under water, come up onto the beach, climb walls. . . it could do anything. This was our original robot. Unfortunately, the engineers, mechanics and scientific geniuses hadn't quite completed it to perfection and the first day of shooting Rover was supposed to go down off the keys into the water, do a couple of signals, a couple of wheel spins and come back up.

It went down in the water and it stayed down permanently. We had Rover in every scene that day and so we had no Rover and Rover didn't look as though he was going to be resurrected at all so we're standing there. . . My production manager, Bernard Williams, wonderful fellow, standing beside me says, 'What are we going to do?' And he looked up and there was this balloon in the sky and he says, 'What's this?' And I said, 'I don't know, what is it?' He said, 'I think that's a meteorological balloon,' and he looked at me and I said, 'How many can you get within two hours?' And he went off and called the meteorological station nearby and I did some other shots to cover while he was away and he came back with a hundred of them.

He took an ambulance so he could get there and back fast 'cause it was quite a ways to the nearest town and he came back with them and there were these funny balloons all sizes and that's how Rover came to be. Sometimes we filled it with a little water, sometimes with oxygen, sometimes with helium depending on what we wanted him to do. We could make him do anything: lie down, beg, anything. We used about six thousand of them. They're very, very fragile."

He hastens to point out that even though happenstance contributed to some of the memorable elements of the series, that these were just little touches along the way on top of the basic concept which was well worked out in advance, and that such little touches along the way like Rover or the Western episode really came about as a result of the creative people already involved in a creative project.

CREATIVITY HELPS

"I was fortunate to have two or three creative people working with me, like my friend who saw the ecological balloon. Where ever one could find these little touches one put them in. But the design of it, the Prisoner concept, that was all clearly laid out. And the style was clearly laid out, and the designs of the set; those were all clearly laid out from the conception of it. There was no accident in that area. You know, the places, the numbers, all that stuff. And the stupid little bicycles. All that stuff."

Regarding the episode "Fall Out," McGoohan was asked if there was conscious religious symbolism in regards to the use of the crucifixion position of the two rebels with their arms drawn apart as well of the use of the song "Dry Bones."

"No, I never had any religious inspiration for that whatsoever. I was just trying to make it dramatically feasible. Certainly the temptation with the guy putting on the thorns and all that stuff; that's Lucifer time, but I never thought of it at that moment. Maybe somewhere in the back of my mind it was there. The hip bone's connected to the thigh bone thing I just thought of as a very good song for the situation and also, it was applicable for the young man because, as you know, it is easy for us to go astray in youth and he was astray and was trying to get everything together again."

Regarding "Once Upon A Time," McGoohan related a curious incident that took place. "That was very interesting because earlier you asked which is my favorite episode and that was probably it. That was one which was written in a thirty-six hour period. Leo McKern, who is a good friend of mine and a fine actor, I think only had short notice to do it, and it really was a two-hander, and brain-washing thing. He was trying to brain-wash me and in the end Number Six turns the tables, and the dialect was so peculiar because all it was 'six, six,

87

six,' and five pages of that at one time.

One lunch time, Leo went up to his dressing room and I went to see the rushes and I went back to his dressing room to tell him how good I thought he had been and he was curled up in this fetus position on his couch there and he says, 'Go away! Go away! I don't want to see you again.' I said, 'What are you talking about?' He said, 'I've just ordered two doctors and they're coming over to this place,' and he said, 'Go away!' And he had, he'd ordered two doctors and they came over and he didn't work for three days. He was gone. He'd cracked, which was very interesting, but thoroughly depressing, and I had to double back on the shots and eventually he did come back and also was in the final episode." But like Number Two in that episode, Leo McKern had a breakdown. In fact, even McGoohan described it as being "exactly the same."

QUESTIONS

When questioned about what he would have done with THE PRISONER if it had been made in contemporary times, McGoohan stated: "I think progress is the biggest enemy on Earth apart from oneself and that goes with oneself; a two-handed pair. With oneself and progress I think we're going to take good care of this planet shortly. They're making bigger and better bombs, faster planes and all this stuff one day. I hate to see it. There's never been a weapon created yet on the face of the earth that hasn't been used. And that thing's going to get used. I don't know how we're going to stop it. It's too late, I think."

When asked if he believed there might be a strong popular reaction against this kind of progress he replied, "No. Because we're run by the Pentagon. We're run by Madison Avenue, we're run by television. As long as we accept those things and don't revolt we'll have to go along with the stream, and the eventual avalanche."

On the subject of how responsible we all are for this and where we became involved, McGoohan explained it this way: "Buying their product, to excess. As long as we go out and buy stuff we're at their mercy. We're at the mercy of advertisers. Of course there are certain things that we need, but a lot of the stuff that is bought is not needed."

As to whether the Village was meant to symbolize something external or internal, within us, McGoohan explained, "It was meant to be both. The external was the symbol, but it is within us all, I think. The surrealistic aspect of it. We all live in a little Village. Your Village may be different from other people's, but we've all got them."

THE REAL ENEMY

Regarding who Number One was supposed to represent, it was posed to him that this was intended to be the evil side of man's nature, was it not? "The greatest enemy that we have. Number One was depicted as an evil governing force in this Village. Who is Number One? We just see Number Two. The sidekicks. Now this over-riding evil force is at its most powerful within ourselves and we have to constantly fight against it. That is why I made Number One an image of Number Six— as sort of 'Ha!' on our ego."

Surprisingly, McGoohan admitted to not knowing who or what Number One would be when he conceived the series. "It had got very close to the last episode and I hadn't written it yet and I had to sit down this terrible day and write the last episode. I knew that it wasn't going to be something out of James Bond, and in the back of my mind there was some parallel with the character Six and Number One and I didn't really know exactly until I was about a third of the way through the script, the last script."

It turned out that even the monkey face which number Six sees when he first unmasks Number One has a point. "Because we're all supposed to come from these things; it's just the same as progress. But the monkey thing, we're all supposed to, according to the theories these days, supposed to come from that original ape, so I just used that as a symbol. The bestial thing and then the other bestial thing behind it which was laughing, jeering and jabbering like a monkey."

Regarding the scene of the grim-faced Number Six driving off in a scene identical with the opening of the series, McGoohan explained that this "freedom" is what the series is all about. "He hasn't got it," he explained, "which is the whole point. When that door opens on its own and there's no one behind it, exactly the same as all the doors in the Village open, you know that somebody's waiting in there to start it all over again. He's got no freedom. Freedom is a myth. There's my final conclusion to it and I was very fortunate to be able to do something as audacious as that with no final conclusion to it because people do want the words The End put up there. Now the final two words for that should have been the beginning."

When asked what sentence or phrase he would like to leave with everyone who watched THE PRISONER, one thing to carry around with them when it was over, McGoohan said that it would be just three words:

"Be seeing you."

"V", a series with a devoted following to this day, began as a creation of Kenneth Johnson when it premiered as a miniseries in 1983. The following year a second miniseries aired, and "V" turned into a full-fledged series. The initial concept was to tell a story similar to that of the Holocaust in a science-fictional setting, with all of humanity finally faced with the sort of deadly violence it has spent millennia inflicting on itself.

In time the focus shifted to a more action-oriented concept, floundering on the same problem that assaults so many original television series: the story cannot be fully told because the story idea is the premise on which the series is based; resolve the story in a dramatically satisfying fashion, and the raison d'être for the series is gone. And so "V": The Series kept dropping back to square one. However, it did this with a certain aplomb which makes it, even now, quite worthy of our attention.

"V", the four-hour miniseries, introduced us to the Visitors. These benevolent aliens appeared with smiling faces and words of friendship and proceeded to dupe the masses of Earth into viewing them as the saviors of mankind. But some humans—notably television journalist Mike Donovan (Mark Singer)— suspect that the aliens are, in a sinister fashion, what Gilbert and Sullivan described as "skimmed milk masquerading as cream." To make matters worse, the seemingly human aliens are actually lizard people with a taste for human flesh! This is discovered by Donovan when he sneaks aboard one of the Visitors' ships and witnesses the revelation of the beautiful Diana's real aspect and observes her partaking of a gruesome between-meal snack.

An underground movement develops—Donovan is joined by Julie Parish (Faye Grant)— and the miniseries ends with resistance building, but with the Visitors still firmly in power. The original miniseries was the brainchild of Kenneth Johnson, a veteran of THE INCREDIBLE HULK series; Johnson wrote, produced and directed the entire thing.

"V" RETURNS

After a year off the air, "V" returned to television with the even more ambitious V: THE FINAL BATTLE. Kenneth Johnson had departed the project and new creative people were involved. While trying to keep the budget in line (the first "V" was reportedly the most expensive TV movie ever made because it went so far over budget), THE

FINAL BATTLE still came out to a whopping 2.3 million dollars an hour for the six hour wrap-up.

The story picks up with the resistance pressing their attacks against the aliens while working on a secret project designed to drive the invaders off the planet. A young girl who had been seduced by one of the Visitors gives birth to twins, one a half-human girl and the other a completely alien form that dies after birth. But the girl child, Elizabeth, begins to mature rapidly, attaining the stature of a ten-year old within weeks. She also seems to have strange abilities that are not common to either human or Visitor.

New members join the resistance, most notably Ham Taylor (Michael Ironside), a former mercenary now devoted to crushing the aliens. He and Mike Donovan share a past and are friendly enemies. Tyler thinks Donovan is too clean cut to be a good fighter and Donovan feels that Tyler is too cold-hearted and merciless.

Robin Maxwell learns that the alien who seduced her and fathered her "children," has been captured. She slips in and finds him contained in a huge cylinder. She takes the red dust, just developed as a weapon against the aliens, and exposes him to it. He dies screaming before any of the others can stop it. Thus Robin exacts her revenge and the resistance learns that their weapon is effective.

Donovan's son had been captured by the Visitors and he wants to stage a rescue before an all-out assault on the Visitors takes place. He succeeds in rescuing him and all across the Earth the forces of rebellion attack. With the help of Fifth Columnists such as Martin—

these are sort of alien conscientious objectors who do not support the aggressive and murderous of their people— even the vast armada of motherships is infiltrated. (Another friendly Visitor, Willie, was portrayed by Robert Englund— better known as the man behind Freddy Krueger.)

The aliens are driven off as the dust is released across the world, making the air unsafe for the reptilian aliens, and V: THE FINAL BATTLE ended on a triumphant note.

THE FIRST SHOW

The series opens just after the invasion has been repulsed, with "The Pursuit of Diana." Donovan spots Diana's attack shuttle and chases her down, forcing her ship to crash. He lands nearby and runs her to the ground, engaging in a vicious struggle with her. She is subdued, apparently due to the intervention of some hunters.

Peace ensues, for a time. Donovan goes back to his television work with his alien friend Martin. Julie Parrish goes to work for Nathan Bates' Science Frontiers, the company responsible for discovering the secrets of the captured mothership. Robin Maxwell takes up residence at a secluded ranch with her father and her Visitor-sired daughter. And a new restaurant, the Club Creole, is opened by Willie.

One year after her capture, Diana is scheduled to go on trial for crimes against humanity. But Nathan Bates, whose Science Frontiers has been entrusted with the captured Visitor mothership, needs the knowledge that someone of Diana's position must have. He cannot pierce the most important secret of the Visitors. Bates hires Ham Taylor, now head of a private security firm, to fake Diana's assassination and kidnap her for him. Tyler agrees with the stipulation that he be allowed to kill Diana after Bates gains the information that he needs. In a secluded shack, Bates holds Diana in a protective bubble, well knowing that she will not attempt to flee since the red dust in the atmosphere would prove fatal to her.

Donovan and Martin manage to figure out what has happened and they track Bates to Diana's prison. Martin has the pills supplied to alien friends of the resistance which offer temporary protection from the red dust. He stays behind while Donovan goes for help. But Martin so wants to kill Diana that he bursts in on his own rather than awaiting Donovan's return. In the ensuing struggle, Martin is injured and Diana steals his last pill. She escapes and Donovan returns only to find Diana gone and Martin dying. He vows revenge and pursues the lizard queen.

Meeting up with Tyler, who is also tracking Diana, Donovan finds her just as she is being rescued by one of her shuttles. Shooting at her proves useless: she sheds bullets off of her thick hide. Diana escapes and the two humans know that only the worst can follow as the Visitor fleet has remained hidden and is waiting on the far side of the moon.

THEY'RE BACK

In "The Visitors Strike Back," it becomes clear that neither Diana nor her lizard rescuers have fallen victim to the red dust. It seems that warm climates render the dust inert after a time, leaving Los Angeles vulnerable. But the attack by the Visitors against Los Angeles proves that the dust does still work, although more slowly. After a time even this fails to happen.

Nathan Bates takes it upon himself to strike a truce with Diana, declaring Los Angeles an open city. His primary incentive: a device that will unleash still-potent quantities of the red dust if Diana does not agree to his proposed truce. Diana, already receiving flak from her ambitious subordinate Lydia and unwanted attention from her superiors, reluctantly agrees. At the signing ceremony, Ham Tyler attempts to assassinate both Diana and Bates but fails.

Tyler finally joins the resistance and aids them in stealing the mothership. They take off to destroy a superweapon being brought into the solar system to end all earthly opposition. Before they pull this off, Elizabeth gives them a bad turn when she wanders off into a cave full of rattlesnakes and forms a cocoon, undergoing transformation. When she emerges, she appears to be about nineteen years of age. While her grandfather, Robert Maxwell, is there to witness this event, Robin Maxwell is in the back country dodging Visitor patrols.

When the mothership is stolen to combat the space platform weapon, Robert Maxwell is mortally wounded. He makes the others flee the ship while he stays behind and pilots it head on into the space platform, destroying the superweapon and the mothership as well. Diana is most displeased.

Meanwhile, Willie the friendly Visitor spots a mark on Elizabeth's hand which he proclaims to be the Mark of Zon, a sign of a prophecy which claims that a child born of both worlds shall someday unite Visitors and humans in peaceful coexistence.

TRUE LOVE

In "The Deception," Kyle Bates, the son of Nathan Bates, enters the picture and falls in love with the shy starchild Elizabeth. This leads him to become involved with the resistance. Meanwhile, Diana schemes to capture Donovan, and, by means of holographic trickery she masquerades as Julie and leads Donovan to believe that the war ended more than a year ago. But a mistake—a newspaper picture of Elizabeth still as a child— shatters this carefully constructed reality. Donovan escapes, thwarting Diana's plan to abduct Elizabeth. The underground's television broadcasts start to feature real-life anchorman Howard K. Smith.

In "Klaus— The Exterminator," Ham Tyler shows Mike Donovan a video of the Visitor's Youth Corps training center, where Sean Donovan, Mike's son, is being brainwashed to be a soldier to fight against humans. As might be expected, the elder Donovan sneaks into the camp and must face down the assassin Klaus (Thomas Callaway), who has been training the young human abductees. Donovan defeats Klaus but cannot rescue his son. Meanwhile, Robin and Elizabeth both develop an interest in Kyle, while Nathan assigns his right-hand man, Mr. Chiang (Aki Aleong) to keep an eye on Kyle, who obviously sympathizes with the resistance.

Visitor disguised technology takes a great step forward in the person of Commander Mary Kruger— who looks exactly like Sybil Danning in a tiger-skin bathing suit. Mary appears in "Visitor's Choice," which focuses on the Resistance's efforts to destroy the Encapsulator, a new device which will radically increase the conversion of humans into food products for the Visitors! Of course the device is destroyed, but not before Julie almost falls prey to it; a good number of Visitor bigshots also go up with the device, including— alas— Ms. Danning. On the domestic side, Nathan Bates has Mr. Chiang punish Nathan after the lad is found stealing explosives, but Elizabeth effects his rescue with her powers.

In "Showdown in Rawlinsville," we get a glimpse into Visitor culture when Diana finds one of her ship's doctors engaging in the pacifistic religion of Zon (the mark of whom apparently appears on Elizabeth's hand, as noted in "The Visitors Strike Back"). This, unfortunately, rates the death penalty, being the Visitor equivalent of Christianity under Nero, and the Zon worshipper is killed in a nasty fashion. Donovan and Tyler attempt to undo the hold of a collaborator who is using forced labor to provide the Visitors with cobalt, an undertaking complicated by an unexpected betrayal.

A ZON WORSHIPER

The title of "Force Field of Doom" pretty much sums it all up; it's a new weapon unleashed by

Diana which could seal off all of Los Angeles. Tyler and Donovan sneak on board the Mothership again, this time to abduct the Visitor who invented the device. He turns out to be another Zon-worshipping Visitor who recognizes Elizabeth's messianic nature and gives his life to undo his destructive creation. Meanwhile, Lydia attempts to inform Diana's superiors of her bungling, but Diana has Lydia's shuttle blown out of the sky.

In "The Christmas Miracle," Diana turns her attention once again to Elizabeth, especially when she learns that the child has undergone a metamorphosis into a young woman. Unable to capture her, Diana is able to get a blood sample and clones her, but the clone turns out to be murderously violent. When the clone tracks down and confronts Elizabeth, it seems to relate to its twin but is slain by a Visitor before any real communication can begin. Or did she give her life to save Elizabeth?

Meanwhile, Nathan Bates finally uncovers Julie's role as a resistance agent, and although she escapes, she fears that Bates has discovered the hideout under Willie's restaurant. In fact, the hideout is blown up, but by the resistance, who then return to the same hideout to rebuild once the elder Bates is convinced that it has been destroyed.

Lydia, Diana's second-in-command, returns unscathed in "The Conversion," bringing with her Charles (Duncan Regehr), an alien who is Diana's superior in rank. When Kyle Bates and Ham Tyler are captured, Charles brainwashes Tyler to kill Mike Donovan when he hears a certain phrase. Tyler is recaptured by the rebels and all is going according to Charles' plan. The rebels have captured Lydia and agree to an exchange of hostages. During the exchange, Nathan Bates speaks the trigger phrase but Elizabeth has sensed that there is something wrong with Ham. She causes a light

> *V told the story of the Holocaust with new trappings, alien lizards standing in for cold-blooded Nazis and this time all of humanity as the target.*

to fall which deflects Ham's aim and he guns down Nathan Bates instead of Donovan.

A firefight breaks out and the rebels escape, reluctantly dragging Kyle Bates along with them even though he wants to remain with his stricken father. Then the power struggle for the open city of Los Angeles begins.

THOSE SNEAKY ALIENS

In "Inquisition" we discover that Nathan Bates is not dead but in a coma. Mr. Chiang runs things in his stead, collaborating even more than Bates did, while a holographic image of the elder Bates remains the public face of power. Chiang has the resistance outlawed and prisoners, including Robin, are taken hostage and set for execution unless Donovan and Julie surrender themselves. They agree and the prisoners are freed in the exchange while Donovan and Julie escape under cover of an ambush. Robin falls under the spell of one of the

95

freed hostages, a handsome young man named John (Bruce Davison) who is actually an alien agent trying to impregnate her to create another human/alien hybrid.

In "Double-Cross!" a wounded Willie is saved by another good Visitor, a doctor (Richard Minchenberg), who tells him that Diana is stockpiling weapons in a hospital— weapons slated for use in a massive offensive against Los Angeles. During a commando raid on the hospital, John's identity is revealed, and he is bumped off by the helpful Visitor physician.

Kyle infiltrates the complex where his father is recovering and learns that although Nathan Bates is conscious, he is not responsible for ordering the reprisals against the resistance. While trying to free his father, Kyle is discovered by Chiang. Chiang attempts to shoot Kyle but Nathan sacrifices himself and blocks the shot. Kyle escapes, vowing revenge. Kyle sneaks back later and surprises Chiang in his office. During the ensuing battle, Chiang is shot and killed. Now the city is wide open for all takers.

After the fall of the puppet Chiang, a full scale human/alien war erupts in Los Angeles in "The Marriage of Charles and Diana," with the aliens searching out and destroying every rebel stronghold they can find. They find the secret base beneath the Club Creole and blast it to shreds, forcing the rebels into retreat. Elizabeth uses her powers to bring the ceiling down and block the aliens who are pursuing them so that an escape can be made.

Meanwhile, the aliens are fighting among themselves. Charles decides to take Diana as his wife so that he can have her sent back to the home planet to bear children. Lydia is not wild about the idea and is very jealous of the situation. The wedding ceremony is held and during it Lydia poisons the ceremonial drink which she knows Diana will imbibe afterwards. But Diana manages to get Charles to take the potion and he is poisoned. When Lydia discovers what has happened she becomes hysterical and Diana orders her arrest.

JUDGE, JURY, EXECUTIONER

In "Trial By Combat," Mike Donovan and Kyle Bates are running weapons to Arizona to supply a resistance group. They encounter a hostile sheriff in the San Bernadino area and escape him through the help of a woman rancher. The learn that the sheriff has been collaborating with the Visitors to supply them with livestock. Donovan stays behind to aid her against the sheriff while Kyle finishes the run to Arizona and returns to Los Angeles by means of a different route.

Meanwhile, Diana has judged Lydia guilty of the murder of Charles and orders her executed. But just as she is about to have the sentence carried out, the Leader's special investigator, Philip (Frank Ashmore), arrives and orders a halt. It will be his judgment as to sentence. He orders Lydia freed pending investigation. Philip, incidentally, looks exactly like the late Martin, being his twin brother. (Why his human disguise should look exactly the same is another matter entirely.)

Following their law, Diana and Lydia both are suspects and Philip orders them to settle the matter in trial by combat. Lydia is doing quite well and is on the verge of killing Diana when Philip calls a halt to the battle. Investigation has revealed that there may be another suspect— another set of fingerprints is on the bottle of poison. Donovan and the rancher enlist the aid of others in the valley and withhold the livestock he wants, thus putting him in bad with the aliens and destroying his power in the valley.

In Los Angeles, a diphtheria epidemic is raging and it is compounded by the ongoing street fighting against the Visitors. The drug needed to fight the epidemic is running low and the only supply is in Visitor hands. Donovan is out of town on a mission; Kyle and Willie enlist the aid of a group of teenagers who are hiding in the hills and harassing anyone who passes through their territory. The gang, called the Wildcats, reluctantly agrees to help, thus giving this episode, "The Wildcats," its title.

MAKING A SWITCH

The raid proves successful but the captured drug proves to be phony. The Visitors knew the raid was coming and substituted baking powder for the drug. There appears to be a spy among the rebels. One of the wildcats is an attractive young woman who takes a shine to Willie, especially after he manages to rescue her from a Visitor. When she proclaims her love for him, he haltingly explains that it cannot be and reveals that he is a Visitor. Horrified, she runs off into the dark of the woods where she falls over a cliff. With the help of Elizabeth, she is rescued, and she apologizes

for reacting to Willie's explanation in the manner that she did.

Julie catches one of the Wildcats communicating with the Visitors. It turns out that they have his younger brother and he is trading information for the boy's release. They tie the boy up and go to meet Donovan at an airstrip where he is bringing the drug needed to combat the epidemic. But the Visitors know where he's landing and plan to surprise him.

The rebels and the Wildcats engage the Visitors in armed combat, gunfire pinning down each side. The Wildcat who has been exposed as a traitor escapes and makes one final valiant statement by crashing his car into the Visitor gun truck, blowing both up. Donovan bails out of his plane and lands safely with the drugs. Thus the epidemic is brought under control and the Visitors have lost one more minor skirmish.

Meanwhile, Lydia and Diana conspire to implicate the ship's pharmacist, Marta, as Charles' murderer, as her fingerprints were on the bottle. Trumping up the evidence, they get her convicted. Her sentence is to be imprisoned in Charles' sarcophagus when it is later ejected into space. Dian insures that the woman is still alive and conscious when the coffin leaves the ship.

DECEIVED

When Diana convinces Philip that Donovan was responsible for his brother Martin's death, the alien leader decides to go after the rebel leader. Diana has an old nemesis of Philip's accompany him— with orders to kill him in the battle so that it will appear that

97

V was a very human show and the fate of its ensemble cast became of great interest to viewing audiences.

Philip and Donovan slew one another. Lydia agrees with this plan. As this unfolds in "The Littlest Dragon," two aliens sympathetic to the resistance flee from the mothership with power crystals vital to operations of the laser weapons, they decide to follow them straight to the resistance.

The aliens, a husband and wife, find Donovan but things become complicated by the female's pregnancy. While she is giving birth in an old warehouse, the Visitors attack. During the battle, Donovan and Philip square off and have a knock-down, drag-out fight, which Donovan wins. But he can't bring himself to kill this alien, who looks just like Martin.

Then Diana's agent steps in, planning to destroy them both, and mentions, in passing, that Diana was the real killer of the turncoat Martin. Before the agent can act, she is gunned down. Philip apologizes to Donovan. Then Philip pledges support and offers to help in any way that he can. He even destroys the power crystals, stating that, "There's already been enough killing." When Philip returns to the ship, Diana is clearly startled to see him alive.

"War of Illusion" involves the Resistance's attempts to stave off a new Visitor weapon, the powerful Battlesphere, conveniently revealed to them by the now-sympathetic Philip. To this end they enlist the services of a computer genius who can counter the Battlesphere with his skills. By coincidence, Lt. James reaches their destination, the home of a Dr. Atkins (MORK AND MINDY's Conrad Janis), before Donovan and his cohorts, having traced some other computer interference to that source. James kidnaps Atkins, not realizing that Atkins' son Henry is the real hacker. Donovan gets to Henry, who redirects the Battlesphere's computerized assault against Science Frontiers, defeats this latest Visitor assault, and saves his dad in the process.

LET THE FEAST BEGIN

In "The Secret Underground," Diana turns her attention to Lydia and has Lydia's brother Nigel transferred to the mothership and increased in rank so that he will be the youngest officer on board. This sets him up as the only possible choice to be sacrificed in a scheduled, traditional feast. At the same time, the rebels steal aboard a ship to find a computer list of the underground leaders hidden by a Visitor sympathizer before he was killed. The resistance must find the tape before the Visitors can locate and play it. The resistance succeeds and Philip halts the execution of Lydia's brother, thus making Diana an even more dedicated enemy as he forces her to stand by him in countermanding the execution.

During a pitched battle between the Visitors and the resistance in "The Return," it looks as though the rebels are about to take a real beating, when all of the Visitor troops are suddenly recalled to their ships. Their Leader is coming and he plans to sue for peace with the humans.

Diana is furious and plots the Leader's demise. The Leader mentally contacts Elizabeth and chooses her to be his mate. This makes the rebels suspicious of the peace initiative but they reluctantly agree because Elizabeth is willing to go along with the marriage. Meanwhile, Willie is meeting his ex-girlfriend Thelma, another Visitor.

Diana disguises two of her men as rebels and when they seemingly blow up the Leader's shuttle, she has them executed prior to questioning. But the Leader wasn't aboard the destroyed craft. Philip had seen to it that the Leader followed in a second ship. Diana and her co-conspirator Lieutenant James are arrested and slated for death.

Elizabeth agrees to leave with the Leader in his shuttle. But just as it takes off, it is noticed that Kyle Bates— a man still in love with Elizabeth— is missing. Did he sneak onto the shuttle to be near her? Since this was the final episode of the series, we may very well never know. And to complicate matters even further, the episode ends with the revelation that Diana has yet another time bomb planted on the right shuttle. What a way to end a series!

"Breakout" was an episode originally intended to have been aired between and "The Visitors Strike Back" and "The Deception," but it was pulled due to violence and was not aired until the rerun season. The show had been moved to a later time slot so younger viewers would not see it. Here, Tyler, Donovan and Robin wind up in a concentration camp ringed by the alien sand sharks known as crivits. Kyle Bates, who had yet to meet Elizabeth, was kidnapped by Diana and used to get his father to turn over the starchild, but the elder Bates could not find her despite his efforts to enlist Julie's assistance.

Tyler and Donovan meet Kyle in the camp and they break out of the prison in a big way.

THE LOST SHOW

Although the "V" series ended with a bit of a cliffhanger, there does exist a first draft of a follow-up episode, which would have presumably opened the next season if "V" had not been canceled.

After further looks at Diana's captivity, the story shifts to the Leader's shuttle, where Kyle emerges from hiding, gun in hand, only to find no one on the craft but the pilot. Elizabeth's disembodied voice speaks to him telepathically, and he is carried away to some sort of other, dark dimension, where he sees the Leader, a huge four-armed lizard being. When he attempts to attack his gun ceases to exist, and Elizabeth appears and explains matters.

Apparently, in ancient times the leaders of the Visitor home world, Saurus, decided to forestall the danger of a too-great concentration of power and broke a mystic artifact called the Anyx, concealing a portion of it on Earth. This, rather than mere hunger, is the real reason for the Visitors' interest in Earth. Now it seems that Elizabeth, by her nature, is a link between the two worlds that can restore the Leader to his full power.

Diana and James manage to escape and take control of the Mothership again, and Lydia decides to go along with this power shift; Philip is denounced as a traitor, and another full-scale assault on Earth is launched.

Donovan, Willie and Julie are imprisoned; Kyle appears in the cell with them; Thelma helps them

99

escape; Julie is vaporized in the escape (!) but the others manage to escape through some air ducts (!!). The survivors disguise themselves as pilots and are aided by Philip when he recognizes them. Diana sees through Philip's pose as their hostage and attempts to destroy them, but Elizabeth keeps appearing on the Mothership and saves them.

PULLING RANK

The Leader keeps interfering with Elizabeth, and she discovers that he is just using her to regain the lost half of the Anyx. She wrenches away from his power and rejoins her friends. All of them but Philip escape in a shuttle; Philip brazens it out by pulling rank on Diana and Lydia. Diana manages to pursue and shoot down the shuttle with the goodguys, which obligingly crashes out of sight and leads her to believe that they are dead. Of course they aren't, and, to top matters off, Ham Tyler shows up and carries them off to rejoin the now-heightened war with the Visitors.

Diana is selected by the Leader to find Elizabeth, for now the Starchild knows his secrets, and has carried off the Syllabus of the Ancients, which holds knowledge which is, unfortunately for her, worded in a very cryptic fashion.

This story would not have ended the series but would have wrapped up the final episode a bit better while leaving the series pretty much the same as it had always been: a chronicle of the war between Earth and the Visitors.

In 1990, a script was written for Warner Brothers for a possible revival of "V" as a syndicated series, which would produce enough additional episodes to fill out the syndication package. This revival would have introduced new characters, given different, more logical, reasons for the arrival of the Visitors on Earth, and essentially completely recast the series. While no new episodes were ever shot, Warner Brothers did attempt to find TV stations interested in carrying the revived "V", along with the original episodes. Not enough signed on. At the time interest in one-hour dramas had declined considerably, ending any chances for a "V" revival.

As it stands, there will always be die-hard fans of "V" who hope someday to see the battle resumed; it will not be forgotten.

In this very Eighties series, a classic legend gets a modern updating and appeals to those who believe that beauty is more than just what we perceive on the surface. Women loved it. Guys tended to get weary of the endless foreplay of the storylines.

BEAUTY AND THE BEAST was created by Colorado native Ron Koslo, a UCLA film school graduate, whose first screenplay sale was for the Sam Neill movie LIFEGUARD. Other films include INTO THE NIGHT and FIRSTBORN, but BEAUTY AND THE BEAST represented his first foray into series television.

The first episode, "Beauty and the Beast," was scripted by Ron Koslow and directed by Richard Franklin (who had directed the feature film PSYCHO II). The saga begins with an introduction to Catherine Chandler, a lawyer who is dissatisfied with her life. She leaves a party unaccompanied and is mistaken for another woman by a group of men who abduct her and take her away in a van. Apparently, Carol— whoever she may be— has been speaking too freely to suit whoever it is that these goons work for. One of them pulls a knife; then we see Catherine being dumped in Central Park. A mysterious cowled figure finds her and carries her inert form away, deep into twisting tunnels beneath the park.

When Catherine comes to, she finds her face swathed in bandages. The voice of her rescuer, Vincent (who remains unseen by the audience, as by Catherine at this point), tells her that she is injured but has been cared for. We also meet Father, whose relationship with Vincent remains obscure. He chides Vincent for bringing the woman underground; apparently Vincent is at some risk out of this subterranean hideaway. But he defends his actions to Father, and in the ensuing days he nurses Catherine back to health, revealing his quiet strength and gentleness. Eventually, she begins to ask questions, and he tells her that he lives in an underground world forgotten by the world above; he himself is a foundling, found in front of a hospital and raised by the man called Father. To occupy her mind, he begins to read Dickens' GREAT EXPECTATIONS to her.

Time passes; the search for Catherine by the police and her father gets nowhere, and Catherine, still blinded by her bandages, begins to grow restless. Left alone, she unwraps her bandages, and receives two shocks in rapid succession: the discovery of the horrible scars left on her face by the thug's blade, and the sight of Vincent's lion-like face in the mirror when he comes up behind her with a cup of tea. She begins to weep, and Vincent runs away, hurt by her reaction to him.

Soon, however, they speak again; Vincent does not know why he is what he is, since he does not know who his parents are. But it is apparent that a bond has developed between Catherine and him, and that once the initial shock of her two discoveries

wears off she does not feel threatened by him at all. He leads her to the surface, and she sees some of his underground world on her way out.

BACK ON HER FEET

Back in the outside world, Catherine undergoes plastic surgery, and months later, her face restored, lands a job in the District Attorney's office, where Assistant D.A. Joe Maxwell is her boss. She also undertakes to learn self defense from a man named Joseph Stubbs. Meanwhile, below the city, it seems that Vincent has been brooding ever since Catherine's departure.

With the help of her co-worker Edie (the obligatory computer whiz who always digs up any information needed for plot advancement), Catherine tracks down Carol, the intended victim of the "warning" administered to Catherine eight months earlier. Carol won't talk to her but takes her card. Later, there is an intruder at Catherine's apartment, and she gets a gun (she's obviously not taking any chances these days!) but it turns out to be Vincent. He is afraid that they cannot see each other again, but this seems somewhat unlikely; much angst ensues before he slips away into the night.

The next day, Carol comes to talk to Catherine at the D.A.'s office. Carol, it seems, worked for an "escort service" operated by a man named Marty Belmont. Belmont's "services" were part of a blackmail racket, and Carol had backed out upon discovering this, which led to Belmont's botched attack on her. Now Carol has come out of hiding and is ready to testi-

fy— but Belmont's men follow her when she leaves the office building and heads for an apartment belonging to a friend of Catherine's. When Catherine goes there, she finds Carol dead. Catherine is also attacked but manages to hold off her attackers.

Meanwhile, Vincent has sensed her danger; it seems that there is some profound aspect to their link to each other. Riding on top of a speeding subway car, he breaks in just in the nick of time as the thugs find Catherine and level a pistol at her. Vincent dispatches them all in a wild fury, only to calm down when he realizes that Catherine is safe. Reunited, they part once more, leaving baffled police to try to figure out exactly what transpired in an empty room filled with the mangled corpses of four hardened criminals.

The next episode, "Terrible Savior," was scripted by noted science fiction writer George R.R. Martin, author of such novels as DYING OF THE LIGHT and NIGHTFLYERS (later made into a movie with the same title). Here, muggers on the subway are being horribly dispatched by a mysterious figure with clawed hands and a significant amount of fur. Remembering how Vincent dealt with the men trying to kill her in the first episode, Catherine is perturbed, wondering if Vincent could be this killer.

CROSSING THE LINE

Catherine's self defense teacher introduces her to Jason Walker, head of a Guardian Angel-type group; they disagree about vigilantism. Catherine is still disturbed, and finally admits her fears to Vincent. He tells her that he is not the subway killer. Investigating further, she talks to Walker, who tells tales of a creature sometimes spotted in the subway. This is obviously Vincent, and some sort of "urban legend" seems to have grown around these few sightings.

Later, the vigilante kills another subway mugger, but also knocks down an innocent old man and severely wounds a policeman. The vigilante slips into the subway tunnels but is spotted by one of the denizens of the Underground. Word is passed to Father and then to Vincent. Vincent visits Catherine again, not knowing that her apartment is being watched by one of Walker's associates. The next day she is abducted and taken to Walker; as might have been guessed by now, he has used the legend to create a figure which he himself portrays.

Now he wants to know about the real monster of the subways. He releases his captive—into the tunnels— and reappears in his "Vincent" costume, trying to pry information out of her with his clawed glove. Vincent once again senses her danger and arrives just in the nick of time. Vincent chases Walker into the caverns and a long battle ensues. Walker gets the upper hand but opts not to kill Vincent; attempting to escape, he plummets to his death in a deep chasm.

The series continued with "Siege," in which Catherine and Vincent fight, each in their own way, to keep a group of senior citizens from being forced out of their homes by greedy and unscrupulous developers. In "No Way Down," Vincent is captured (for the first time) by a gang; the drama that unfolds around this involves the retarded brother of the gang leader, who shows Vincent some kindness, but is killed. A horribly battered and beaten Vincent escapes and eventually dispenses some fairly sharp justice.

George R.R. Martin returned as script writer with "Masques," a tale set at Halloween. Vincent uses the holiday as a means of walking freely through the surface world. He goes to a party also attended by Catherine and her father; the party is in honor of Brigit O'Donnell, an Irish peace activist. Vincent falls into conversation with Brigit; the two of them seem to be on the same wavelength on the subjects of peace and violence. Meanwhile, a man dressed as a clown crashes the party and begins to follow them into the park. When Vincent senses the clown, who has a gun in his hand, he knocks him out.

WHO TO TRUST?

Catherine, meanwhile, has been trying to catch up with Vincent but is being accompanied by a man named Pratt. When she sees him, he walks away silently. Pratt identifies the clown as an IRA agent named Michael O'Fay, who was part of a plot to kill Brigit. Pratt himself is an Interpol agent out to foil the plot. They all get into Pratt's car, only to discover that O'Fay was actually sent to protect Brigit and to take her to her dying father; he had his gun out only because he didn't know if the man in the lion mask was a threat or not. Pratt is really the assassin, named Jamie Harland, and his victim is to be Brigit's father. He kills O'Fay first, since O'Fay had killed

Harland's brother, and then Harland, Brigit and Catherine go to the hotel room of Brigit's father.

Meanwhile, Vincent has— surprise!— sensed that Catherine is in danger! As he makes his way to her, Harland prepares to make Mr. O'Donnell watch his daughter die before his own death. Vincent does not arrive at this point, however— it is Catherine who uses her martial arts training to disarm him! The gun lands on O'Donnell's bed, and he prepares to kill Harland, but Brigit stands in front of her father and demands that the killing stop. This works on him but not on Harland, who takes Brigit hostage at knifepoint. Now Vincent shows up, dispatches Harland, and slips away. Brigit resolves to reconcile with her father, and Catherine leaves them alone. Vincent rejoins her and they walk together through the city until dawn, when a jogger, commenting on Vincent's costume, reminds them that the night when two worlds can mingle is over.

"The Beast Within" reunites Vincent with Mitch, a childhood friend and former denizen of Underground. They had become estranged when Mitch became involved in surface crimes and was not allowed to hide out in Father's domain. This intertwines with a tale of dockside labor violence, in which Mitch is deeply involved. Vincent is captured again in "Nor Iron Bars A Cage,' this time after a college professor, Hughes, spots him in a badly-focused photograph. He hopes to prove this discovery to his skeptical colleagues, and captures Vincent with the aid of a grad student, Gould. The two men disagree; Hughes thinks their captive is human while Gould believes oth-

erwise, an opinion bolstered by Vincent's willful refusal to speak. Hughes hears Vincent speak while dreaming of Catherine, but Gould does not, and tranquilizes Vincent.

Meanwhile, Catherine spots an article in a sleazy tabloid paper about an old woman who witnessed the capture of a strange man-beast through her balcony telescope! While she looks into this angle, Hughes moves Vincent to another location to get him away from Gould. Realizing that Hughes is not a threat like Gould, Vincent speaks to him, and tells him that he will die if he is not set free.

ON THE TRAIL

Catherine finds the tranquilizer darts used to catch Vincent and traces them to Hughes. She confronts the scientist, who is about to release Vincent, when Gould steps in and struggles with Hughes, stabbing him. Catherine gets the key. Gould tries to get it from her but foolishly comes close enough to the cage for Vincent to snap his neck. Hughes dies but not before making his peace with his former prisoner; he had hoped to restore his tarnished academic career with this astounding discovery, but realizes that he was wrong to imprison another thinking creature.

Father's past is revealed in "Song of Orpheus" when a message reveals that his long-lost love has returned to New York. The woman, Margaret, draws him to the surface, but he winds up being charged with the murder of her lawyer. Margaret is dying of cancer, and is being hounded to hand over her fortune to Henry, a man whose charitable causes are really a scam. In police custody, Father won't talk except to deny that he killed the man, and recalls the 1950s, when he was a physicist who questioned the government's conclusions regarding radiation hazards. For this he was branded a Communist and blacklisted.

Catherine is informed of Father's disappearance by Vincent and does some research, eventually unearthing Father's history as well as his name: Dr. Jacob Welles. Vincent discovers an old letter among Father's things: it is from Margaret. She and Welles had actually married only to have their marriage annulled by her father after Welles' disgrace. She tracks down Margaret but can't get past Henry, who has Margaret drugged. She then goes back to work and spots Father in a cell when she goes to jail to take another prisoner's deposition. Afterward she speaks to him and tells her about Margaret. He tells her that the dead lawyer was a friend who had helped him back in the fifties.

That night Catherine takes a look around in the dead lawyer's office but is abducted by Henry. The lawyer had been on to Henry's scams, but this knowledge is of little use to Catherine as Henry intends to kill her. Vincent of course is on his way to rescue her, which he does quite dramatically by ripping off the top of an elevator and carries her off up the cables! Henry's plan is foiled, and Father is able to spend Margaret's last week of life with her.

MORE STORIES

"Dark Spirit" involves Catherine in strange voodoo-like goings on which threaten her life. In "A Children's Story," Catherine and Vincent converge, from different levels, on a seemingly legitimate children's home which is actually supplying a Fagin-like character with unwitting soldiers in his street army of crime. In "An Impossible Silence," a mute teenage girl witnesses the murder of a cop by other cops who are on the take and involved in drug traffic. The girl, Laura, is an Underground dweller. Meanwhile, a black suspect (the real killer was white) is arrested, and Catherine has a seemingly airtight case against the man. But she must believe Vincent when he tells her that the man is innocent. Laura must ultimately decide to go aboveground to testify; she must leave the security of her world in order to save the suspect, and in the end decides to pursue a life on the surface.

"Shades of Grey" finds Father and Vincent trapped in a cave-in; the undergrounders unite to save them but their fate depends on an ingenious youth who has been ostracized by the community. In "China Moon," two young lovers from the Chinese community flee social strictures into the Underground, which is then invaded by the Tong forces of the father of the man who intends to marry the young woman. Apparently,

The television series retold the classic story in modern terms. The message was still the same: appearances are not important.

there is a bit more knowledge about Underground in Chinatown. But with his world facing invasion from above, Vincent offers a fierce defense, and the lovers are free to marry and live below ground.

"The Alchemist" introduces the villain Paracelsus, who has been distributing a deadly drug on the surface, and taking only gold as payment. Clues lead Father to realize that Paracelsus is behind the plot; Paracelsus was largely involved in carving out the haven of the Underworld but was banished by Father years before. He still lives elsewhere under the city; in fact, Father confronts him and warns him that his actions might draw attention to the subterranean world. It is obvious that Paracelsus is envious of Father's position of authority.

Meanwhile, aboveground, Catherine is involved in official attempts to trace the source of the drug, which lead to the death of a cop on the case. Below ground, debate rages: all feel that Paracelsus must be stopped, but Father stops short of sanctioning the only means that can accomplish that end: killing the alchemist. Taking matters into his own hands, Vincent tracks and confronts Paracelsus but falls victim to the drug, which acts on contact. He goes berserk and attacks Father. Eventually Catherine finds him and calms him.

HEART OF GOLD

Vincent finds Paracelsus again and tells him to leave the city. They begin to fight when a fire blazes up. Paracelsus is about to rejoin the fight but turns to save his gold and is engulfed by flames.

"Temptation" finds Catherine's boss, Joe, framed on drug charges (to get him off a case) while Vincent seeks a gift for Catherine for the first anniversary of their meeting. Another former friend of Vincent's returns in "Promises of Someday"; this time he is a man named Devin who left their world years before. Under the name of Jeff Radler, he begins working in the D.A.'s office with Catherine on an important case.

He also seems to know about the underground city, and Catherine observes him go to the entrance. His identity is revealed; Vincent is happy to see him, but it is obvious that there is a deep rift between Devin and Father. Part of this stems from the fact that Devin is not really a lawyer; a highly intelligent man, he has worked many jobs the world around, always an impostor! He even delivered a baby while posing as a doctor— by caesarian section! Catherine wants him to clear out of the D.A.'s office, which he promises to do.

Eventually, the truth comes out: Father actually is Devin's father. At last they are reconciled, but Devin leaves again to another part of the world. This time he travels under his real name— Devin Welles. And Catherine discovers that his work on their case was actually good enough to make the charges stick.

In "Down To A Sunless Sea," Catherine meets an old flame who she dropped because of his possessiveness; he manages to win her trust, somewhat, but he's actually deranged and obsessed. Years before they had mused about a country home; Catherine has forgotten that, including her off-hand comment about how nice a red stove would be, but he has remembered every detail. He gets her to come along with him to look at a house he's thinking of buying— but he's already bought it, and that red stove. As far as he's concerned, they're home now, and there's nothing she can do about it. Fortunately, Vincent has spent the entire episode coping with a recurring dream about running through a forest, and once again rescues Catherine. He narrowly avoids killing the crazed suitor, who winds up in a mental institution.

ENDING SEASON ONE

"Fever" finds the inhabitants of Underground turning against each other when a treasure trove is discovered there. "Everything Is Everything" involves Catherine in Gypsy justice. "To Reign In Hell" brings back Paracelsus, whose scarred face is partially covered by a mask of molten gold. The alchemist strikes back by abducting Catherine, and Vincent must gather a band of friends to go deeper than any have ever ventured underground in order to save her. Paracelsus' monstrous helpers are slain, as is one of Vincent's friends, but the villain escapes.

"Ozymandias" finds Underground threatened by the foundations of a giant skyscraper. "A Happy Life" is a contemplative episode where Catherine assesses her life; action-free, it brings the first classic season to a thoughtful conclusion.

The second season of BEAUTY AND THE BEAST veered into more soap opera like territory and began to falter in the ratings. Towards the end, Paracelsus returned to truly tax Vincent, revealing skills as a shapeshifter and offering revelations about Vincent's past that might be lies— but might not be. He even impersonates Father— a great scene for Roy Dotrice— and tests the dark side of Vincent's character.

To further complicate matters, the call of feature films lured Linda Hamilton away from the show, and the character of Catherine was killed off, leaving Vincent to work solo in the faltering episodes of the short final season. Thus, the promise of the series, so bright in the first year, sort of faded out quietly in the end, not with a bang, but a whimper.

BEHIND THE CHARACTERS

Linda Hamilton, who played Catherine on BEAUTY AND THE BEAST, was born in Maryland. She began acting at an early age, eventually attending the prestigious Lee Strasberg Theater Institute. After finishing these studies, she worked for a time on the soap opera SEARCH FOR TOMORROW. She moved to California in 1979 and began to work in films. Here, she appeared in Stephen King's CHILDREN OF THE CORN, KING KONG LIVES, BLACK MOON RISING, and, most significantly, THE TERMINATOR. And of course, in the aftermath of BEAUTY AND THE BEAST, she achieved her biggest success, and major stardom, with Arnold Schwarznegger in the massive hit movie TERMINATOR II.

Ron Perlman, who essayed the crucial role of Vincent in

109

BEAUTY AND THE BEAST, was primarily a stage actor. Born in New York, he studied stage extensively, and appeared in such Broadway stage productions as "American Heroes," "Pal Joey," "Tartuffe," "Measure for Measure," "The Iceman Cometh," "Two Gentlemen of Verona," and "House of Blue Leaves." He appeared in such movies as QUEST FOR FIRE, ICE PIRATES, and, most notably, THE NAME OF THE ROSE, where he came to the attention of the producer of BEAUTY AND THE BEAST. His role as the deformed hunchback, Salvatore, certainly displayed his skill at working under heavy makeup, and helped convince the BEAUTY AND THE BEAST team that he was the man for the job.

The character of Father was portrayed by British actor Roy Dotrice, who first began acting while a teenage prisoner of war of the Germans in WWII . During his nearly four years of incarceration, his captors had the POWs take part in theatrical productions, so one could say that Dotrice was literally forced into the theater. After the war and his liberation he returned to England and pursued his stage career, eventually becoming a member of the Royal Shakespeare Company. In time, Dotrice found stage work on the other side of the Atlantic, and, in addition to that acclaimed work, managed to make a living off of American television as well, appearing in such network fare as REMINGTON STEELE, MAGNUM P.I., HART TO HART and THE A-TEAM. Finally, he landed the role of the patriarchal Father on BEAUTY AND THE BEAST.

Catherine Chandler's boss on BEAUTY AND THE BEAST, Deputy District Attorney Joe Maxwell, was played by actor Jay Acovone. A native of New York state, Acovone started out on such soap operas as SEARCH FOR TOMORROW and AS THE WORLD TURNS, before a 1985 move to the West Coast began leading to other television work. These included shots on the short-lived series version of DOWN AND OUT IN BEVERLY HILLS, on Fox's WEREWOLF and on Andy Griffith's MATLOCK. He also appeared in the Dan Curtis produced miniseries WAR AND REMEMBRANCE, as Maselli. His feature film work includes appearances in the Al Pacino feature CRUISING and the horror movie 976-EVIL, directed by Freddy Krueger himself, Robert Englund.

Catherine's friend and confidant in the D.A.'s office, Edie, was portrayed by Ren Woods, an Oregon native who first got into show business as a singer at the age of nine, actually joining Bob Hope in Vietnam as part of a singing group at the age of fourteen, and eventually landing the role of Dorothy in the West Coast company of "The Wiz." For television she has appeared on HILL STREET BLUES, THE JEFFERSONS, and in the groundbreaking miniseries ROOTS. On film, Woods has appeared in such movies as John Sayles' THE BROTHER FROM ANOTHER PLANET, CAR WASH, JUMPIN' JACK FLASH and the Alex Cox film WALKER, all the while maintaining her career as a singer.

The main villain of BEAUTY AND THE BEAST, Paracelsus,

was portrayed by the actor Tony Jay. The British born actor ruefully recalls that George Lucas actually approached him to play the part of Obi Wan Kenobi while STAR WARS was still in the embryonic stages, but he never heard anything more about the project from Lucas and eventually discovered that Alec Guiness had wound up with the role. But long before that slice of fame eluded him, Tony Jay had always kept acting in his life, although generally in an amateur capacity, until a move to South Africa led to his involvement in radio dramas and a little bit of film work. Seven years later he returned to England, forty years old and obliged to resume his career at ground zero.

While intergalactic fame eluded him, he did luck into a part in the international stage hit "Nicholas Nickleby," which also aired on PBS stations. This Dickens adaptation led him right into opportunities for American television, as it did for the actor who played Nickleby, Roger Rees, who played tycoon Robin Colcord for several seasons of Cheers. Tony Jay's first American television gig was a pilot called CIRCUS which never got off the ground but did lead to Jay's marriage to his make-up artist! After that, roles on HUNTER, THE GOLDEN GIRLS and the short-lived HILL STREET BLUES spin-off BEVERLY HILLS BUNTZ quickly ensued, as well as parts in the theatrical films TWINS and MY STEPMOTHER IS AN ALIEN, where he finally got to play an Obi Wan Kenobi-like character. And of course, then came the part of Paracelesus on BEAUTY AND THE BEAST.

When the series was cancelled, a handful of episodes had not been aired but these were quickly seen when the Lifetime Channel picked up the show for syndication. Although there were rumors that Linda Hamilton was forced to leave the series, she actually left due to the lure of feature film work. The way her character was brutally killed off, after giving birth to Vincent's child, angered many longtime fans. Only a few episodes of the revised version, which introduced a new love interest for Vincent, aired before CBS pulled the plug. Although rumors abound of a BEAUTY AND THE BEAT motion picture which would reunite Ron Perlman and Linda Hamilton, this project has never advanced beyond the rumor stage.

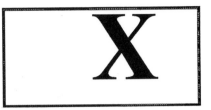

They said it wouldn't work. Even died-in-the-wool STAR TREK fans— especially them—foresaw a quick and ignominious death. But Gene Roddenberry was determined to do it again, and he succeeded, as THE NEXT GENERATION has hardily survived its creator and is well into the middle of its sixth season.

It was a rough start for THE NEXT GENERATION. Would people come to accept a bald-headed Frenchman with a British accent as captain, a woman doctor, a logical android (too much like Spock, said some) and a Klingon as key members of the Enterprise crew? Time has shown that the answer to this question was a resounding yes. Despite the halting quality of the early episodes of the series, STAR TREK—THE NEXT GENERATION persevered, despite such weight as an extremely plodding pilot episode.

As the pilot, "Encounter At Farpoint," begins, Captain Picard (Patrick Stewart) has just been posted to the new Enterprise (NCC 1701-D). He doesn't even have a first officer yet, but is taking the ship to Farpoint Station to pick him up. The second-in-command, Riker (Jonathan Frakes), is a key character in Roddenberry's re-visioning of things. Whereas Kirk would beam down to any hostile planet despite the risk, Starfleet protocol (and centuries of historical precedent) dictates that the commanding officer of a vessel not place himself at risk.

Rumor also has it that Roddenberry opted for this approach because of his experience with the classic Trek, where his dream of a true ensemble was somewhat unbalanced by a certain actor's constant efforts to keep the focus of the show on his character. Now the function of that character is divided into two: the older, wiser man in charge and the more rakish, daring first officer.

The second episode, "The Naked Now," was a virtual remake of "The Naked Time." It reveals a few things about the characters, but not much, beyond demonstrating just how annoying Wesley Crusher could be. "Code of Honor" continued this distressing string of similarities to the old show. "The Last Outpost" introduced the Ferengi, the new villains, who don't make much of an impression in their initial foray. They were actually too clownish to pose much of a threat, and their offhand remark about how disgusting it is that the Federation makes their women wear clothing makes it impossible to find them anything but amusing.

GENDERLESS

"Where No One Has Gone Before," reflecting the new show's lack of gender bias, used Wesley fairly well and introduced the Traveller, an alien who, after a fashion, becomes one with his own mathematical equations and casts the ship into distant unexplored regions of space. This episode demonstrated that the special effects of THE NEXT GENERATION were prepared to go where no one had gone before even if the

scripts weren't quite ready to make the trip.

"Justice" condemned Wesley to death for violating a seemingly trivial taboo on a planet of blonde fitness fiends. It demonstrated that Picard could give speeches which were more long-winded and dramatic than even Capt. Kirk at his best when he was talking a computer to death. "The Battle" provided information on how Picard lost his old ship the Stargazer in a battle with Ferengi; the old nemesis he defeated then shows up with revenge on his mind. For a show with everywhere to go, the episode reveals a lot less about Picard than one would imagine.

"The Big Goodbye" introduced Captain Picard's passion for hard-boiled detective fiction, as well as the holodeck concept. While Picard is off playing Dixon Hill, private eye in a simulated 1940s San Francisco, a malfunction causes the characters in the program to develop real personalities. . .and real bullets in their guns. This episode won the coveted Peabody Award for television excellence due to its unusual ideas on the nature of life and reality. The series hasn't come close to winning the award since, even though much better scripts have come down the pike.

"Datalore" is an evil twin story enlivened by Bret Spiner's dual role of nice and not-so-nice androids. It clears up some of the mystery of Data's origin, but not much else. It does demonstrate that Spiner is an actor to watch, even when forced to play a one-dimensional villain.

Things picked up with "Heart of Glory," the first episode to focus on Worf as more than just

a grouchy guy who's handy with a phaser. Renegade Klingons fleeing from the Empire try to involve Worf in their rebellion, provoking a serious conflict of interest for him.

HEATING UP

The show suddenly gets relevant in "Symbiosis," in which the medicine one planet provides to keep another from dying of an ancient plague is revealed to actually be a highly addictive drug. A typical Roddenberry classic, in that the issue-of-the-week kills the story and leads to some windy dialogue.

"Skin of Evil" kills off Tasha Yar rather offhandedly, then gives her a nice funeral. The episode was written by Joseph Stefano, the writer/producer who contributed much to the first year of THE OUTER LIMITS. This episode features a being who's been exiled to a planet for his evil deeds but we learn precious little about what made him that way. Again, just another one-dimensional TV villain.

"Conspiracy" reveals that the Federation has been infiltrated by evil bugs from a distant galaxy, but Picard gets to the bottom of it and finally gets to use a phaser on someone in the series. This remains the only NEXT GENERATION episode to bear a viewer advisor for violence due to the state-of-the-art exploding head special effects, the first of their kind to appear in a made for television project. Some fans were more than merely surprised by the gruesome finale.

The first season wound up with "The Neutral Zone," an oddly uncompelling episode involving 20th Century Terrans who experience future shock after being revived from cryonic suspension. The Romulans reappear, probably since the Ferengi were a washout as heavies, but the show's ending is weak and inconclusive, and the season just sort of fizzled out. It would be quite some time before we figure out that this episode is a subtle harbinger of the introduction of the Borg.

The second season of THE NEXT GENERATION showed a marked improvement over the first. In the season opener, "The Child" is conceived upon Deanna Troi by an alien entity which wants to learn about humans by becoming one. The resultant offspring grows at a rapid rate, but must abandon its physical body when it realizes that it is the source of the deadly radiation affecting the safety of its new-found family. A touching if manipulative story, this one gave Marina Sirtis plenty of emotion to work with.

TURNING OLD INTO NEW

Rewritten from a script originally intended for the once-planned STAR TREK II TV-series, this episode introduced also two new characters: Guinan, the wise and ancient bartender of Ten Forward (played by Whoopi Goldberg), and Dr. Pulaski (portrayed by Diana Muldaur) as a replacement for Gates McFadden and Dr. Crusher. Guinan would become a long-standing part of the series; Pulaski, an ill-conceived attempt at a Bones-like character, would, although ably acted by Muldaur, fail to last more than one season, when Gene Roddenberry reversed his arbitrary decision to fire Gates McFadden.

In "Elementary, Dear Data," Geordi programs in a holodeck adversary worthy of— in a crucial slip of the tongue— Data, which makes Moriarity a match for the android, who is playing Sherlock Holmes. The professor, now "real," begins to learn about the Enterprise, and eventually kidnaps Dr. Pulaski in a ploy to be granted life outside the holodeck.

"The Outrageous Okona" veered into idiocy as Data tried to learn about humor from a 20th Century standup comic created by the holodeck. Joe Piscopo guest starred, leading us to believe that this is how the future would view standup comedy of the 1980's. One shudders at the concept.

"The Schizoid Man" was in fact Data, his personality impinged upon by a brilliant but dying scientist who sees the android as his ticket to immortality. The arrogant scientist cannot carry off the masquerade in silence and is soon revealed; getting him to relinquish his second chance at life is another matter entirely, but when he realizes the harm he's done he returns control to Data and gives up the ghost, as it were.

"Unnatural Selection" not only subjects Dr. Pulaski to an aging disease like the one in "The Deadly Years," it solves the problem using the transporter matrix— the same solution used in a similar episode of the animated STAR TREK series. The only real suspense comes from the difficulty in finding a transporter trace for Pulaski, as she avoids using the device at all costs. Diana Muldaur does a fine job in the only episode that does her character any justice at all.

115

A NEW BALL GAME

Now that the Federation and the Klingon Empire are friends, it seems inevitable that an officer exchange program should be initiated; in "A Matter of Honor," Riker gets first shot at it and jumps at the chance. Here he must learn to eat Klingon food, fend off the advances of Klingon women, and betray his captain. . . this last as a matter of duty, of course. A fascinating look at the Klingons, imbedded in a genuinely suspenseful plot. This remains the only Klingon episode not to revolve around Worf. It also shows that Riker isn't quite so bland and easy-going when placed under pressure.

"The Measure of a Man" is essentially a courtroom drama in which an ambitious science officer, intent on disassembling Data to see how he works, questions the android's rights as a sentient being, provoking Picard to mount an eloquent defense (with a little help from Guinan).

"The Emissary" is K'Ehleyr, a half-human Klingon woman, who embarks on a tumultuous romance with Worf while trying to help the Enterprise rendezvous with a shipload of Klingons about to revive from cryonic suspension. Arriving too late, Picard is faced with a group of Klingons who still think there's a war on. Worf and K'Ehleyr pull off a masterful ruse: the Klingons could never accept that the Federation won the war, so they trick them into believing that the Empire was triumphant. Worf assumes command of the Enterprise for this brief but crucial period; deception is an accepted and honored Klingon method of facing a challenge.

The season fizzled out with a bargain-basement episode, "Shades of Gray." Riker, infected with a deadly virus, dreams scenes from past episodes. How convenient for the budget. Pulaski saves him, of course, in her last stand as attending physician on the Enterprise. This is a weak, if not downright pathetic, conclusion to a season which improved immeasurably over the first season. Almost any other episode— "The Emissary" or "A Matter of Honor"— would have seen the season out with a bang rather than a whimper. Still, the show had more than overcome the founderings of its first season, and had proven that it could stand on its own. The next season would be even better.

THIRD TIME IS A CHARM

The third season got off to an adequate start, and would prove to be THE NEXT GENERATION's best season yet. Repenting of his dismissal of Gates McFadden, Roddenberry brought back Beverly Crusher as the Enterprise's Chief Medical Officer. No mention was made of her tenure as head of Starfleet Medical and Pulaski was not even referred to; her whereabouts were left unknown. There was one good scene, though, as Wesley and his mother deal with the fact that she'd been gone for a year.

With these changes in place, the third season revved up with "Evolution," involving one of Wesley's science projects gone awry, as microscopic nanites begin to eat the computer core of the Enterprise. A scientist preparing to

116

observe a rare stellar event is perturbed by this interference and tries to kill the by-now sentient creatures, provoking their displeasure. But with Data as an interface, communications are established and things are ironed out to the benefit of all involved. This episode, written by Michael Piller, marked his introduction to the series. He soon became Executive Producer and eventually went on to co-create DEEP SPACE NINE with Rick Berman.

In "Ensigns of Command," Data is assigned to get a human colony off a planet before the aliens with legal rights to that world arrive and destroy them. We actually get to see Data get down and dirty when he displays his willingness to lay waste to the colony in order to prove his point.

"The Survivors," a human man and his wife, occupy a small patch of green on a planet otherwise utterly destroyed by an alien attack, and have no desire to be rescued. This is a touching story dealing with love and grief and introduces an alien race unknown before and not seen since, in spite of their omnipotence. John Anderson, who died in 1992, demonstrated what a truly fine actor he was.

"Who's Watching The Watchers" casts Picard as an unwilling god when a Federation observation post on a developing world is discovered by the inhabitants. Picard finally beams down to explain that he's only human, but his would-be disciple refuses to take even this at face value. This story deals with the impact of religion on a culture and whether it's important or not.

WORFING

"The Bonding" is another key Worf episode. When a member of an Away Team commanded by the surly Klingon is killed, the guilt ridden Worf feels responsibility for the woman's orphaned son. So does an alien entity on the planet involved, which tries to assuage the boy's loss by recreating his dead mother. The story actually explores the boundaries of grief and the way it affects even those not directly involved.

"The Enemy" finds Geordi stranded on a hostile planet where he must overcome a wounded Romulan's suspicions and gain his trust in order for them both to survive. It's an old idea recycled here to good effect. "The Price" details negotiations for a potentially valuable wormhole; Riker's poker playing skills lead Picard to make him the replacement negotiator, but the real danger at the table is a secret Betazoid misusing his powers to gain an edge as well as to romance Deanna Troi. Although this attempts to broaden the character of Troi, all it does is demonstrate how basically uninteresting she is as we find it difficult to care that she's having such a good time with this guy.

"The Defector" is a Romulan admiral determined to prevent a sneak attack by his

STAR TREK: THE NEXT GENERATION admirably continues the concepts of the original series while adding its own unique touches.

Empire. Naturally, Picard doubts his story, and it turns out to be a Romulan ploy to capture a Federation ship, but the admiral was sincere, having been used by his own government. It does a lot to establish some personality for the Romulans and elevates interest in them considerably.

"The High Ground" involves Picard and Beverly Crusher in a terrorist/ hostage situation; the terrorists have legitimate grievances but go too far, as does the oppressive government in combating resistance. An intriguing story that loses force by trying to straddle both sides of a difficult and emotionally charged issue. This was the episode Roddenberry hinted at early in the series when he spoke of wanting to cover the issue of terrorism from the terrorist's point of view. It makes a small attempt at that but ultimately has Dr. Crusher lecturing the terrorist leader on the futility of what he's doing. The fact that he dies at the end tends to only punctuate her speech.

Q-ING UP

Q shows up, stripped of his powers by his peers, in "Deja Q." Picard takes some convincing that Q is not responsible for his current crisis, which involves a moon with a decaying orbit. Q learns humility of sorts when an old nemesis of his shows up and threatens the Enterprise; he leads it away in a shuttlecraft, and is awarded with the restoration of his powers for this selfless act. Needless to say, his humility dries up pretty quick, but he does save the planet threatened by its moon, forces Picard to listen to mariachi music, and enables

Data to enjoy a good laugh, an attribute which for some reason has never been repeated since.

"Yesterday's Enterprise" introduces a temporal distortion which casts the Enterprise-D into an alternative history where the Federation is losing a long running war with the Klingons. Tasha Yar plays a key role in this drama, and sacrifices her life to restore the proper time-line. Many fans regard this as not only the best episode in the entire six year history of THE NEXT GENERATION, but the best STAR TREK episode in the entire twenty-five year history of the series.

"The Offspring" is Lal, an android 'daughter' created by Data. This is a very touching episode, but suspense is introduced by having the Federation attempt to take her away for study, as in "The Measure of a Man," as if the legal precedent set there had no weight. Picard is willing to risk his career to protect the androids' rights, but the issue becomes moot when Lal malfunctions and dies, after having developed the emotions her 'father' lacks. This marks the directorial debut of Jonathan Frakes, who handled the sensitive emotions of this tale with great aplomb.

In "The Sins of the Father," the Enterprise crew is in for a rough ride when a Klingon exchange officer temporarily assumes Riker's duties. Worf learns that the Klingon is actually his younger brother, who reveals a secret: when Worf and his parents went to the outpost later destroyed by the Romulans, the younger brother was left behind, presumed dead by the Empire but actually raised by another family. He has sought out Worf after all these years because their late father has now been accused of helping the Romulans' notorious attack, and only the eldest son can challenge charges of treachery in the High Council. Otherwise, the stigma of a traitor will be borne by their family for seven generations. One further catch: if Worf's challenge fails he will be executed. Plot elements in this episode will lead to the season four finale.

R AND R

"Captain's Holiday" leads Picard into trouble and romance, thanks to Riker's mischievous suggestion intended to make the vacation a bit more interesting. Time travellers, Ferengi and the beautiful if unethical archaeologist Vash provide the staid captain with a week he won't forget, although he doesn't get much reading done as per his original plan.

"Tin Man" is the name given an alien artifact, apparently a sentient spacecraft. Tam, a Betazoid born with full powers is assigned to make contact. His telepathy, untempered by slow development, makes it hard for him to avoid the constant mental chatter of most beings, but he becomes friends of sorts with Data, whose mind is closed to him. This script has an interesting history as it was submitted by two freelancers who saw it sell and go into production within thirty days, an almost unheard of series of events.

"Hollow Pursuits" introduces the potentially sticky subject of holodeck abuse, as Barclay, one of Geordi's engineering team, uses the deck to vent his frustrations and explore his fantasies, using his superior officers as characters in his creations. It demonstrates that not everyone aboard the Enterprise is quite as ordinary as we'd been led to believe. Thankfully this character has appeared as a central figure in at least two episodes since then, both dependant on his personality quirks.

In "The Most Toys" Data is kidnaped (and his destruction faked) by an avaricious collector. Although intrigued at being filed alongside a Roger Maris baseball card (complete with recreated bubblegum odor), Data will not comply with his captor's wishes until a woman is threatened. The villain in this episode was originally played by David Rappaport, but when the actor attempted suicide, he was replaced and all his scenes refilmed with the new actor. Rappaport's performance was reportedly one of his finest as he played the villain as being even more menacing than the version we saw.

Spock's father "Sarek" appears in this episode which bears his name, but his vital diplomatic mission is threatened by an encroaching form of senility, rare among Vulcans but overwhelming when it strikes. This story demonstrates just how good an actor Mark Lenard is and how neglected he has been by Hollywood in recent years. It remains the best script he has been given to work with in the actor's entire twenty-five year experience with STAR TREK.

ENDING WITH A BANG

After the dismal and cheating conclusion to season two, THE NEXT GENERATION's producers wisely chose to end the third season with a bang-up finale. "The Best of Both Worlds" brings back the Borg,

119

The changes from the first series mirror our reality. Thus "no man" becomes "no one".

intent upon absorbing the Federation and all other life forms into their machine-hive mind. The story ends with Picard captured, turned into a Borg— forcing Riker to give the order to fire on the Borg ship, Picard and all! While the ending is extremely contrived to be just what it is—a season finale—the episode overall is quite good and holds up well in repeated viewings.

The cliffhanger ending left audiences clamoring for more, which was a shrewd move after the two lame-duck season finales that preceded it. It was a long summer after "The Best of Both Worlds" brought the season to its end; there was little else for captivated viewers to do but to watch reruns of THE NEXT GENERATION until fall.

"The Best of Both Worlds, Part Two" opened the fourth season and successfully matched the quality of the first part, kicking off another consistently good season. In a rare example of a television science fiction series dealing realistically with the probable fallout from a dramatic situation, the very next episode, titled "Family," written by Ronald D. Moore and directed by Les Landau, deals with the less spectacular side-effects of the battle with the Borg. In it Jean-Luc Picard chooses to take a well-earned shore leave on Earth, which they had come close to in their battle with the menace from beyond our galaxy. The Enterprise, still docked for repairs, remains in orbit over Earth.

For the first time in twenty years, Picard returns to his home in France. While Picard is physically recovered from his ordeal, he still has psychological scars to contend

with and has chosen to wrestle with these problems by returning home and seeing his brother again. Unresolved conflicts with his brother still remain, but Jean-Luc is prepared to confront these if necessary. His older brother, Robert, is a farmer bent on keeping the family traditions alive. Robert has always regarded Jean-Luc as arrogant and ambitious. This comes out when Jean-Luc arrives at the family estate and meets his young nephew, Rene. The boy remarks that Jean-Luc doesn't look arrogant. So even before meeting Robert we know he has a grudge against Jean-Luc. When Jean-Luc meets his brother for the first time in nearly twenty years, Robert barely says hello and acts distant and preoccupied.

SEEING GREEN

Robert is Jean-Luc's older brother and appears to be in his sixties, but he still works in his vineyard. Over dinner, a small argument develops in which Robert complains that "Life is already too convenient" when the talk of getting a food synthesizer comes up. When Rene remarks that he won a ribbon for his paper on starships, Robert is clearly annoyed. The boy has already remarked to his uncle that some day he's going to be a starship captain, too. Jean-Luc gets along well with Robert's young wife, though, as well as with their son, Rene. But Robert himself remains distant and critical.

The portrayal of Robert Picard is strange because it's the 24th century and yet he acts like a 20th century man railing against "progress." The thing is, life would be so different in the 24th century from what it's like today that no one in living memory would remember what it had been like in "simpler" times. The more simple times would have been hundreds of years ago. This one aspect of Robert Picard's character does not ring true, but it can be overlooked in light of the more important issues the episode deals with. In an effort to give some perspective to Robert Picard, Jean-Luc's old friend Louis remarks at one point that Jean-Luc was always reaching for the future while Robert was reaching for the past.

In the vineyard they finally get to the bottom of their resentments as Jean-Luc tells Robert that he was a bully and challenges the older man to try and bully him now. Robert lashes out at his brother and a fight erupts. They roll around in the vineyard until they're covered in mud, at which point they break out laughing. Jean-Luc's laughter soon gives way to tears, for he has been unable until now to face the self-doubt raised by the Borg's use of him.

"They took everything I was. They used me to kill and to destroy and I couldn't stop them. I should have been able to stop them! I tried so hard, but I wasn't strong enough. I wasn't good enough. I should've been able to stop them!" Now that his emotions have broken through, he can begin to deal with them. Robert points out that Jean-Luc will have to live with this for a very long time, whether below the sea with Louis or in space on the Enterprise. Jean-Luc makes his decision and decides to return to command the Enterprise.

YOUTHFUL WISHES

As Jean-Luc prepares to return to the Enterprise, young Rene once more expresses his desire to be a starship caption. In Rene, Jean-Luc sees himself when he was a boy; a child whose eyes were always on the stars. Robert has realized this as well and has had to come to terms with the fact that his son will undoubtedly follow in his uncle's footsteps, not his father's. Even after Jean-Luc has left, Rene sits outside staring up at the stars. His mother remarks, "It's getting late." But Robert replies, "Let him dream." Both brothers have come to terms with what the future holds.

"Family" is one of the best episodes NEXT GENERATION has produced, and the fact that it has the courage to deal with human issues on a human level rather than on a galactic one makes it all the more compelling. We understand these people and how each has affected the other, for better or for worse. And each of them has to come to terms with the emotional fallout from that. The episode also has two subplots, one involving Worf's human foster parents visiting the Enterprise and the other with Wesley watching a hologram of his father for the first time which was made at the time of the boy's birth. But try as they might, these subplots just seem like distractions from the infinitely more interesting story of Jean-Luc coming to grips with his personal demons and reconciling with his brother.

Sadly, this is supposedly one of the lowest rated episodes THE NEXT GENERATION produced, and yet it is far and away one of their top ten entries. At the

121

very least it should have been nominated for the Humanatus Award, the annual prize given to television writing which promotes strong human values. Perhaps had it dealt entirely with Picard and dispensed with the padding of the minor subplots it would have received more serious consideration.

"Brothers" opens with Data suddenly shifting into a mysterious mode and taking over the Enterprise, diverting it to a mysterious planet, and beaming down, leaving a bewildered crew striving to figure out the complex code he entered into the computer—using Picard's voice! On the planet's surface, Data encounters an aged human who turns out to be Dr. Noonian Soong, Data's creator, who has long been presumed dead but who actually fled the events described in the first season's "Datalore" and escaped to this distant hideout.

INTRIGUING EPISODES

"Reunion" brings back Worf's gal K'Ehleyr and continues the Klingon saga. A Klingon cruiser hails the Enterprise. Worf's old flame K'Ehleyr beams over with a message for Picard: the leader of the Klingon High Council is dying, and wants Picard to discover which of the contenders for his position has been poisoning him. K'Ehleyr also has a surprise for Worf: their original encounter years before produced a son. In the course of this action-packed tale, K'Ehleyr is killed by Duras, and Worf dispatches Duras is a good old-fashioned Klingon revenge— but his discommendation still stands.

"Future Imperfect" finds Riker awakening after sixteen years

to find himself the captain of the Enterprise, with a son. He has forgotten the sixteen years in question; his last memory is of a visit to a planet, where he was infected by a virus that lay dormant for years until wiping out all memories accrued since its inception. In the Philip K. Dick tradition, apparent reality takes several sharp turns before the truth is revealed.

Another episode, "The Wounded," was also an intriguing story. While surveying a sector near the space of Federation enemies-turned-allies, the Cardassians, the Enterprise is fired on by a Cardassian ship. After a brief exchange of fire, Picard discovers that the peace has been broken by the Federation ship Phoenix, commanded by Ben Maxwell. Maxwell has been out of communication for some time, and is apparently acting on his own initiative: the Phoenix has destroyed a Cardassian science station without provocation. The Federation orders Picard to investigate, and to take a Cardassian team aboard as observers. This episode introduced the Cardassians, an alien race who would play a larger part in the storyline of "Ensign Ro" in season five and particularly in the backstory of DEEP SPACE NINE.

ONE OF THE BEST

"First Contact" breaks with the series format to provide a startling look at the questions raised by the Federation's techniques of determining a planet's worthiness to join. Here, we see the Enterprise crew as aliens, from the Malkorian's point of view. In is one of the finest episodes in the six years of THE NEXT GENERATION as introduces a truly original approach never before taken in STAR TREK.

In "The Host" Beverly Crusher finds romance with a handsome alien ambassador only to find that the fellow's mind and personality reside in a sluglike being that uses a humanoid host body as a vehicle— when the host body dies. A good sport, Crusher transplants the being into Riker, temporarily, so that important treaties can be negotiated. Complications ensue when the love-struck ambassador pursues Beverly—with Riker's body! She eventually gives in to him, but draws the line when his new host body arrives and turns out to be female. Crusher is, after all, just an old-fashioned girl. The obvious question— how does Riker feel about all this?— remains unanswered.

"Redemption" is finally made available to Worf in this fourth season finale, but under rather trying circumstances. The story, a rather convoluted but intriguing account of Klingon power politics, ends with the restoration of Worf's family name— but he also leaves Starfleet to aid his brother. And Denise Crosby turns up as a Romulan!

The fifth season, sorry to say, would see a considerable variability in the quality of NEXT GENERATION episodes. The fifth season starter, "Redemption, Part Two," continued the established tradition of season-opening sequels, wrapping up Worf's Klingon sojourn as Picard strives to end Romulan interference in Klingon politics. Denise Crosby's character is revealed to be the daughter of Tasha Yar, by way of the time-slip factor of "Yesterday's Enterprise,"

but Picard overcomes his surprise at this and the day is carried, with Worf returning to Starfleet.

"Ensign Ro" introduced Michelle Forbes as Ensign Ro Laren, a troubled character whose initial abrasiveness would be toned down to a wry sarcasm in subsequent appearances. Avoiding the squeaky clean characters who populate the Enterprise, she's drafted out of a prison cell where she'd languished after a Federation courts martial. Her character quickly emerged as one of the most interesting to appear in any version of STAR TREK.

WHEN ALL FAILS, BRING IN SPOCK

With "Disaster" it became painfully apparent that THE NEXT GENERATION's fifth season might not be as good as the two preceding it; a space disaster disables the Enterprise, with such cliched results as: Picard is trapped in a turbolift with a group of children! Keiko goes into labor and Worf must help with the delivery! On the positive side, it was well played, with good comic moments, and it at least managed to keep the childbirth and elevator plots separate.

But the big selling point of the fifth season was to be the two-part "Unification," in which Leonard Nimoy would appear as Spock! The first half had an intriguing set-up, with Spock appearing at the end after Picard and Data have trailed him to the Romulan homeworld. But the second half fell flat, standing perhaps as little more than a commercial for

123

the forthcoming feature STAR TREK VI. Part one of "Unification," in which Spock only appears at the end, actually remains the better of the two-part story, showing that while the presence of Leonard Nimoy may deliver boffo ratings, it doesn't mean that he can save a hastily written script. [The script was conceived in August 1991 and aired in November, leaving precious little time for rewrites and reconsiderations.]

Close on the heels of "The New Ground," (Worf having trouble with his new role as a dad), the kids-in-space theme of season five kicked into high gear with "Hero Worship," in which a traumatized boy attempts to subdue his troubled emotions by emulating Data's android behavior. This Data episode is remarkably well written and shows the good drama that NEXT GENERATION is capable of at its best.

"The First Duty" brought Wesley back or, rather, Picard visits Starfleet Academy, where Wesley has messed up seriously. An interesting episode, and one which shows us Picard's Academy mentor, the crusty old gardener Boothby— portrayed, in an intriguing science-fiction television crossover, by My Favorite Martian star Ray Walston! After five years, THE NEXT GENERATION finally granted that Wesley Crusher is a human being capable of making mistakes. Some mistakenly felt that Wesley was disliked by many fans just because he was a teenager, when actually it was because Wesley was consistently portrayed as being cute and perfect.

YOUTH POWER

In "Imaginary Friend" this season's focus on children rears its ugly head again with yet another kid story, this one involving an alien entity which brings a little girl's imaginary friend into actual existence— but which perceives the adults on board the Enterprise, especially Picard, as the girl's enemy, and wreaks a bit of havoc before Picard explains things and order is restored.

Even the Borg get exposed to the recurring youth angle in "I, Borg," when a damaged adolescent Borg is rescued and learns something about humanity and individuality, another annoying 'underneath, we're all the same episode even though the Borg has been raised in an alien environment and was never exposed to humans until found by the Enterprise.

The fifth season reached its dubious conclusion with "Time's Arrow," which appeared, from the coming attractions, to flirt with being the "Data's Brain" of THE NEXT GENERATION. Data's head, centuries old and quite dead, is discovered in a mysterious cavern excavated under San Francisco, and the Enterprise investigates the mystery, eventually sending a team, including Picard, back to nineteenth-century California. However, it was actually an interesting episode, creating and sustaining a strange mystery involving 24th century aliens plundering 19th century Earth.

The sixth season opened with the dismally pointless conclusion to "Time's Arrow." The writers on hand seemed utterly incapable of doing anything with the intriguing mysteries presented in the first half; the plot fizzles, giving the cast little more to do than wear period costumes. To pad out the tale, an inordinate amount of screen time was given to having Mark Twain wander around the Enterprise and spout off various spurious Twainisms. In the end, Data's body (brought back through time) is reattached to his head (now five hundred years older than the rest of him.) The padding in this, and any story, is apparent in that all of the scenes with Mark Twain can be excised without affecting the plot one way or the other. He just takes up space.

The next episode, "Realm of Fear," found Barclay back in the focus, having anxiety attacks about using the transporter and finding strange creatures in the matter stream when he finally takes the plunge. Not an amazing episode, but perhaps the best written of the sixth season to date as the mystery is unguessed by viewers until the moment it's solved, and the cleverness involved works quite well. But for the most part, this season has maintained a remarkably high level of mediocrity.

IF NOT SPOCK, THEN SCOTTY

The next episode, "Relics," featured the return of James Doohan as Scotty. Seems a ship with Scotty crashed in a remote region of space, and he rigged a feedback cycle in the transporter which keeps his pattern intact for seventy years or more. Some amusing moments as Scotty's earnest attempts to help out start to get on Geordie's nerves, but there's no surprise when the two engineers

team up to find the solution to the latest threat to the Enterprise.

Best moment: Scotty's incredulity upon discovering that when the captain asks how long a repair will take, Geordie tells him exactly how long it really will take, instead of inflating the time required.

Most glaring omission: Scotty is taken aback to discover how much time has elapsed, but he doesn't even ask what has happened to any of his former crew mates. Some of them must be dead— or can we anticipate eventually finding everyone who ever appeared on STAR TREK trapped in some sort of time suspension? Let's hope not! This episode pulled high ratings, promising that Scotty, and possibly other old Enterprise crew people, will not remain out of sight for long.

In "Rascals," Picard, Guinan, Ensign Ro and Keiko (Mrs. Miles O'Brien) are caught in a transporter accident (this season's favorite plot device, the transporter) and return as children—obviously a fifth season story held over a year. Mentally, they're still adults, but Picard soon relieves himself of duty and hands command over to Riker due to the peculiar nature of his affliction. No sooner is this done than the Enterprise is taken over by Ferengi pirates in stolen Klingon vessels. Among other things, they herd all the children together as hostages— including the victims of the transporter snafu. No need to explain any further— that Picard uses his adult wits and his stature to outwit the Ferengi, recruiting Alexander (a.k.a. Worf Junior) into the plot.

A GOOD SHOWING

Round this out with "The Quality of Life," a lame Data episode (Data discovers that cute robots of the SILENT RUNNING variety are actually sentient) and a Wild West holodeck episode (Worf, Alexander and Deanna are trapped in the holodeck when Data's attempt to interface with the ship's computer goes awry and turns all the holodeck characters into him— yep, it was called "A Fistful of Datas") and there's little concern that the show is now on its holiday hiatus. If only there were a STAR TREK feature to distract us at this point, as there was during the fifth season (where, admittedly, THE NEXT GENERATION had an extra-long hiatus while STAR TREK VI was in release).

It should be pointed out that the cast of THE NEXT GENERATION is not at fault here. They are as good as ever, as are the production values. But the writing— well, where is the writing? Have all the good story ideas been diverted to Rick Berman and Michael Piller's forthcoming spin-off DEEP SPACE NINE? Or has the talent simply been diffused too much by the preparations for that series?

The series now seems incapable of rising above a certain level of mediocrity. Perhaps THE NEXT GENERATION is winding down. Perhaps (some hope) it will revive itself when new episodes begin airing once more in early 1993. But whatever the case, STAR TREK— THE NEXT GENERATION has certainly had its share of truly superb stories to tell, and it is these— stories like the ongoing Klingon drama of Worf's family history, and individual episodes like "The Drumhead," "A Matter of Honor," "Who's Watching The Watchers," "Family," and "First Contact," among other classics— which will stand as the legacy of THE NEXT GENERATION.

After a decade since Glen Larson's science fiction disasters,

NBC was willing to give it another try.

Few subjects in science fiction have gripped the imagination as surely as the concept of time travel. The possibilities which present themselves when one considers the challenge of moving between the moments is almost impossible to quantify. On television the subject has been touched on from time to time, usually with simple-minded results

QUANTUM LEAP takes exactly the opposite approach. Narrowing the focus of the journeys down to the last half of the Twentieth Century, the stories deal less with the obvious and more with the personal aspects of a point in time, and the most successful episodes are those in which we've come to care about how it turns out.

Some people have called this a science fiction show for people who don't like science fiction. Certainly this isn't what the average person thinks of when the words science fiction are mentioned. It's not STAR WARS, STAR TREK, BUCK ROGERS, BATTLESTAR GALACTICA or SPACE RANGERS. It's both earthbound and yet unbound by the ordinary restrictions of time and space. It's about a world which is both familiar and unfamiliar, where many things are possible and often we're kept guessing right up until the next Leap takes place.

QUANTUM LEAP premiered as a mid-season replacement series on March 26, 1989. The two-hour premiere opens with Al stopping on a lonely stretch of road to give a woman whose car has broken down a lift. But no sooner does he do this than he sees a distant glow lighting up the night sky, and as his state-of-the-art 1999 sports car blasts off down the road, he phones the complex and discovers that Dr. Sam Beckett has activated the Quantum Leap accelerator which will pitch him back in time.

Although not established in the pilot, Sam activated the project prematurely due to impending plans by the government to pull the plug on the project because it hadn't produced any results yet. This was the same scenario which powered events in the pilot for THE TIME TUNNEL back in 1966. Beyond that, the shows have little in common.

THE FIRST LEAP

QUANTUM LEAP is just as likely to present a comedy as it is a drama, and sometimes does a little of both. In the opening episode, Sam wakes up in 1956 and barely remembers his own name. What he does know for certain is that he's not a test pilot for the X-2 in spite of what his pregnant wife tells him. Sam is further confounded when he goes into the bathroom to shave and the face looking back at him in the mirror is not his own. This is where things get confusing.

TAKING A

QUANTUM LEAP

Although everyone sees the person Sam has become in the past, it's actually Sam who is there. We sees Sam and so does Al (Dean Stockwell), an associate on project Quantum Leap who is projected into the past with Sam, but only as a hologram. Al's real body remains in the future, in 1999, where the Quantum Leap Project is located. The physical body of the person Sam is replacing also is in the future but the person has little memory of what happened to them when they return to their own time.

As Bellisario explained it, regarding where the people go when Sam is living their lives, "They're in the waiting room, which is a medical looking room. Very antiseptic, with people in white garments or robes, all enclosed and examining them and probing them and checking them; a lot of strange lights, futuristic. And when they leap back, they immediately think that they have been kidnapped by aliens. And if you check, that's when it all started, y'know, right about the time Sam started leaping. All these encounters of the third kind began to happen. They were all quantum leaps."

The confusing part, and where science seems to stretch into sorcery, is the offhand explanation that people don't see Sam in the past, they see the person Sam has replaced because that's who they expect to see! There's some double-talk about auras and other such things, but it was a long time before I understood that Sam's body was in the past, not just his mind. Sam invariably appears in the life of someone who is either in danger or is in the position to save the life of someone he knows.

This next aspect is even more of a stretch. An unknown force, sometimes referred to as fate or destiny or a higher power, is guiding Sam from one leap to the next. Each time Sam must set things right, usually by preventing a death or some other grave injustice and thereby changing someone's life for the better. In the pilot he's just guessing that this is what he has to do. It was a theory that he and Al had discussed.

COMPUTER AIDED LEAPING

When Al appears, he has a handlink device which puts him into direct contact with a computer nicknamed Ziggy. Ziggy provides the background information on the people Sam is involved with in that time period, which gives him the deadline he's working against. In the pilot he's in 1956 in the form of a test pilot who is destined to die in a plane crash. His pregnant wife will deliver a premature baby which will be stillborn. As luck would have it, Al is a former pilot (in a later episode we learn that he was shot down over Vietnam and was a prisoner of war for several years). Al directs Sam how to fly the X-2 and enables Sam to break Mach Three (three times the speed of sound) and eject safely even though the plane crashes. Since Sam has several degrees, he uses his medical knowledge to prevent his "wife" from delivering the baby prematurely, thereby saving the baby's life.

The balance of the pilot has Sam appear in 1968 in the form of a baseball player who scores a winning run and saves the careers of himself and his coach. The most dramatic part of the episode, though, is when Sam remembers his father's name and phones him, pretending to be the son of his father's brother. Sam's father died in 1972 and so he is able to say things to his father he never had the chance to do in life. When the call ends Sam is weeping. Too often television shows portray the hero as being a macho lout to whom a display of tender emotion would be unheard of. But Sam is portrayed as a realistic human being whose own feelings and emotions become very much a part of the events he lives through. It's this aspect which tends to save stories which otherwise seem to stretch credibility rather thin.

QUANTUM LEAP was created by Donald Bellisario. Bellisario had worked in television for several years prior to creating this series, and had written scripts for such shows as AIRWOLF, MAGNUM P.I., QUINCY and TALES OF THE GOLD MONKEY. He was tired of that and wanted to do something which was completely different from the typical action shows which populated prime time. Having just completed work on the feature film LAST RITES, he wanted to turn his attention to something lighter in tone.

"I was trying to look for a format that would give me an opportunity to do a completely different kind of show," Bellisario explained. "I wanted to be able to do an anthology. Television networks and studios don't want to do anthologies because people really don't watch them and they're very hard to syndicate so that they can recover their money. I just wanted to do something that would have a different story to tell every week."

A SHOW IS BORN

The writer/producer had been toying with the idea of doing something mystical which would be set in the southwest. And while he was working out these ideas in his head he read a book called COMING OF AGE IN THE MILKY WAY by Timothy Ferris which deals with scientific concepts written about in a way that laymen can understand them. One of the things the book dealt with was the concept of time. These ideas came together and out of them was born QUANTUM LEAP.

Even though he didn't think he could get a network to go for a time travel show he was determined to try just the same. The hook which he determined would make it easier to sell was that the main character would only be able to travel within his own lifetime. Sam was born in 1953 and so that would be the furthest back he could go, but since the last half of the twentieth century has been a very volatile period in history, this still left open a wide array of story possibilities. Although at the time the series first aired, Bellisario promised, "It will never be November, 1963 in Dallas, Texas with Kennedy coming to town. I don't want to do that kind of show. I'm more interested in doing a show about people and relationships."

Bellisario pitched the idea to Brandon Tartikoff, who was then the head of NBC programming. Tartikoff agreed that the idea was a different one, but he liked it. It was original and yet it was easy to understand. Tartikoff's measure for a successful show was that he had to be able to explain it to his mother in less than twenty seconds. If it was more complicated than that then he felt that viewers might find it too complicated to follow as well. While on one level this seems amusing to hear, on another it's sad as it explains the state of much of the programming on television today. It has to be dumbed down for the viewers, or so the networks feel. This is why the new science fiction series SPACE RANGERS is just cop show scripts dressed up with aliens and spaceships.

QUANTUM LEAP is the first television series to stipulate that time can be altered—that it is not immutable. On the other hand, it also seems to be saying that there are not any drastic consequences of these alterations. Once Sam has altered the past successfully, Al is able to tie into Ziggy and discover the outcome—always positive. It's when Sam cannot change the past that bad things result, including the recent episode in which Sam's actions almost resulted in Al being executed for murder in the Fifties, thereby altering Sam's own future. The people Sam helps, the lives he alters, are always the little people. He brings rewards to lives where there had been tragedy before.

BOTH GOOD GUYS

What insures that Sam's actions will only have positive results is the character Scott Bakula portrays. Dr. Sam Beckett isn't just a brilliant scientist, he's also a man of morals and convictions. He has vowed not to use the past for personal gain, such as investing in a small company in the Fifties which will become a billion dollar corpo-ration in the Sixties and Seventies. He helps people better their lives through their actions, not their investments.

Scott Bakula became interested in acting in 1974 when he was attending the University of Kansas. While he had started out intending to get a law degree, he switched to the theatrical department. He left college in 1975 and briefly appeared in a touring company of "Godspell." He then worked for awhile painting house and as a loan officer for the Household Finance Company before working on Broadway. He appeared in such productions as "Marilyn: An American Fable," and appeared off-Broadway in "Three Guys Naked From The Waist Down." He also acted in the Boston and Los Angeles productions of "Nite Club Confidential."

The actor began getting work on television in such programs as MY SISTER SAM, MATLOCK and ON OUR OWN. He also had a recurring role in the early episodes of DESIGNING WOMEN as Mary Jo's ex-husband, the obnoxious gynecologist. Bakula also appeared on the short-lived series GUNG HO and EISENHOWER AND LUTZ.

On the big screen he had a supporting role in SIBLING RIVALRY as the husband of Kirstie Alley. He had the starring role in NECESSARY ROUGHNESS as a former star high school quarterback who goes to college twenty years later and joins the football team. Bakula credits the wide range of performances he's been called on to give as the reason he was offered his film roles. On QUANTUM LEAP, besides playing ordinary people, he's also played a hitman, a rabbi, a school teacher, a pregnant woman, a chimpanzee and a Klansman.

RELATIONSHIPS IS THE KEY

Bakula was cast in the role after Donald Bellisario contacted the actor's agent and sent two sample scenes from the script. The actor describes the show as sort of a cross between BACK TO THE FUTURE and PEGGY SUE GOT MARRIED, and describes it as being a people show as opposed to a hardware kind of science fiction show.

"It's easy to get distracted with what you might perceive to be the technicalities of the show—the computers and all," he told STARLOG. "If you really want to get into discussing the time travel and quantum physics and all those theories, you could get lost. To me, it's a show about relationships—somebody who finds himself in a strange place and gets involved with the people that are there in his life. And this guy becomes kind of like a classic American hero and he cares about the people and he does good things because he wants to do them."

Dean Stockwell, who plays Albert, is a former child star who made good. He began acting at the age of six, and in the Forties he appeared in such films as ANCHORS AWEIGH and THE BOY WITH GREEN HAIR. In KIM he acted opposite Errol Flynn in one of that actor's last major films. By the time he was sixteen, he was fed up with Hollywood. He felt that he didn't have a life of his own and was working all the time, so he quit the business. For five years he worked at odd jobs and just worked at being himself without having to answer to anyone.

By the time he was twenty-one he was ready to return to Hollywood. In the late Fifties he re-established his career in "Compulsion" on Broadway. In the Sixties he dropped out again, becoming involved in the Hippie movement and the Haight-Ashbury scene. The second time he tried a come back, it was much tougher. Not until landing a role in the 1982 film PARIS, TEXAS did his four-

The paradoxes and intellectual games inherent in time travel form an underlying element of QUANTUM LEAP.

teen year exile from Hollywood truly come to an end. That was thanks to a recommendation by an old friend, actor Harry Dean Stanton. He then appeared in the low budget film TO KILL A STRANGER, followed by a prestigious role in the big-budget David Lynch film DUNE.

A FUTURE OF HIS OWN

Stockwell heard that a film version of DUNE was in the works, and being a fan of the book, he managed to secure a meeting with David Lynch. Initially all the roles had already been cast, but when the actor slated to play Dr. Yueh left the project, the director offered the role to Stockwell. Lynch liked working with Dean Stockwell so much that he cast him in a small but pivotal role in the controversial film BLUE VELVET. Other film

133

roles followed sporadically, including BEVERLY HILLS COP II, GARDENS OF STONE, TO LIVE AND DIE IN L.A., TUCKER and MARRIED TO THE MOB. Initially Stockwell's role in MARRIED TO THE MOB was supposed to be spun off into its own series, but it never came together. It was Stockwell's humorous character in MARRIED TO THE MOB that brought him to the attention of Donald Bellisario.

In describing QUANTUM LEAP, Stockwell states that, "It's a fantastic concoction, really. Albert, my character, which is embellished as the series goes along, has lots of facets. He's obviously a brilliant guy. He was a physicist, an astronaut and is a colorful person who obviously still enjoys life. He's also interested in other people's problems and does everything to help them.

Regarding the casting of these two actors, Bellisario stated, "When Scott came in and read, I didn't want to say right on the spot, 'Oh, boy, you're the guy,' and get all excited and he'd go wild and ask for eight million dollars. But he came in, he read, he walked out, and. . . it was the first time I'd met Scott. And I said, 'He's perfect. This is the guy.' And then when I heard Dean would be interested in doing it, I was really excited. Dean came in and read and he was the character. He was just there. And it was wonderful. And it's been that way ever since. These guys are just great to work with. Non-star stars. By that, I mean no attitude on either one of them. They're just there to work and have fun. And the whole set reflects it. It's just a lot of fun."

The earliest episodes were pretty routine—Sam leaps into someone's life and helps change it for the better, but they're pretty interchangeable, even when Sam finds himself in the role of a Mafia hitman. But in episode six, "The Color of Truth," Sam finds himself a black man in the pre-civil rights south of 1955. It deals with the obvious questions of civil rights as his character tries to convince people that things cannot continue the way they are. It plays things pretty safe even if its heart is in the right place.

SECOND CHANCES

The best episodes of QUANTUM LEAP dealt with human issues which were determined to truly get to the heart of the matter. None were better at this than episode thirty-one, "The Leap Home." When Sam appears on November 25, 1969, he finds himself not in another stranger, but in his own body at age sixteen. Sam is overwhelmed at being able to see his family again as his father died of a heart attack in 1972, and his brother, Tom, was killed in Vietnam.

Sam decides on his own that he's there to save his father and brother. But when Al tells him that he's actually there to win a basketball game he'd previously lost, because of all the people this will positively benefit, Sam rejects that as being too simplistic. A basketball game? Sam is determined to help his family. He tries to convince his sister, Katy, that he knows what will happen in the future by singing her a John Lennon song which won't be written for several years. She becomes frightened and

Sam tries to tell her it was just a joke.

When he tries to help his father by getting him to change his diet, his father becomes angry because Sam is telling him that the food he raises on the farm is bad for him to eat. His father is just too set in his ways to start eating healthy now. Sam tries to convince his brother that when he's in Nam, that on April 8, 1970 he'll agree not to go out in the field on any missions. Sam goes out and wins the game, but just before he leaps, Al tells him that Tom still dies in Vietnam. When Sam leaps he finds himself in Vietnam, in the body of one of Tom's fellow soldiers on April 7, 1970.

The following episode, titled "The Leap Home II, Vietnam," has Sam succeed in saving his brother's life. In this storyline we see Sam get angry over his situation for the only time, feeling that after all the good he's done for others, the higher power or whatever is controlling his time traveling destiny owes him something in return. In part one it seems that all he's granted is the chance to spend a few days with his family before it was ripped apart by tragedy.

In part two, Sam succeeds in saving Tom's life, although seemingly not only at the cost of the life of a journalist who didn't die before, but also by losing a chance Sam might have had to rescue Al right after he'd been made a P.O.W. in Vietnam. Al says it's okay because he was released five years later, and he was always free in his mind. This episode is more complicated than many of the others and deals with more delicate moral and philosophical issues.

STILL HOPPIN

Episode Thirty-Five, "The Boogieman," is a strange episode. It's a dream story, except at the end when Sam wakes up in time to save the life of a handyman. In a brush with history, as Sam occasionally has in his travels, a nerdy kid named Stevie King is inspired by some things Sam says to try his hand at writing horror stories. This originally aired October 26, 1990 and was a Halloween episode. It is effective, though, as we wonder what's going to happen next when Al turns out to be an impostor who's really a demon angry at Sam for setting right what the demon had originally caused to go wrong. Dream stories are usually annoying but this one is much more clever than most.

While some shows start to wind down by the time they hit fifty episodes, QUANTUM LEAP has only started to wind up, trying new ideas rather than staying with the tried and true. In the fourth season opener, something goes wrong and Sam and Al switch places. Al winds up as the leaper, with gaps in his memory as to who he is and what he's doing, and Sam is back in project Quantum Leap, inside the imaging chamber where he is now the hologram guiding Al.

It's June 15, 1945 and Al is in the body of a soldier who's just returned from WWII. By episode's end, Sam has to save the lives of two people (including Al) and try to get their situation straightened out. In the same season, Sam plays a rape victim (a woman) in 1980 and a research chimp in 1961. The latter episode deals with the animal rights issue—by taking both sides in the story although the scientist

135

QUAN T U M L E A P addresses controversial subjects, including gay rights and prejudice.

portrayed decides to end his cruel animal head trauma research at tale's end.

The fourth season also produced an even more controversial episode. When word got out that an episode would have Sam leap into the body of a gay high school student, everyone started jumping up and down, including NBC who threatened not to pay for the episode. It seems that other shows which had featured gay characters had suffered pullouts by sponsors fearful of product boycotts by fundamentalist and right wing groups.

Although Bellisario claimed he wouldn't back down, the teenage characters were advanced into military cadets and the storyline dealt less with discrimination than with someone being falsely accused of murdering the gay cadet. It turned out that the cadet had actually committed suicide and framed an inner circle of gay bashers in the academy. Sam succeeds in preventing the cadet from killing himself. Whether the character Sam plays, who is the gay cadet's roommate, is gay is left up in the air as Sam ultimately decides that it doesn't make any difference whether he is or not.

TOUGH ISSUES

The one place where the episode doesn't pull back is when Al reveals that he's very upset with the concept of a gay military cadet and he and Sam debate the subject. So even though the storyline was watered down somewhat, it still confronts the issue of homophobia by making it a personal issue between Sam and Al. The fact that Al has an extensive military background makes his reactions believ-

able rather than contrived. With recent real-life headlines, their debate is even more timely.

The fourth season finale is easily one of the best episodes in the entire series. While the show generally tries not to get too complicated for fear of alienating the non-science fiction enthusiasts, the finale pulled out all the stops and made the audience either pay close attention, listen, or leave the room confused. When Sam leaps into Al's body in the Fifties, they at first are uncertain what Sam has to do. Al was wrongly accused of murder at that time but was cleared. But when Al isn't cleared, Ziggy reveals that Al is in danger of being tried, convicted and executed.

When Sam fails to come up with a solution before a certain moment, the odds against Al being freed become overwhelming and suddenly Al is gone—replaced by a different hologram assistant played by Roddy McDowall. It's a brilliant scene. The show becomes even more complicated as multiple time leaping is done to not only save Al, but save a woman who was Al's alibi and who later died in an accident. This time she doesn't die and Al's not only freed, but the real killer is caught.

It's a complex web of storytelling which must be seen to be believed. It deals with the dangers of paradox in time traveling, which until then the series had shied away from just because of how complicated and confusing it can be to confront. Bellisario confronts it head on in a complex yet logical manner. It's a story filled with surprises which just pile one on top of the other and make it impossible to guess the outcome. A real class act.

BENDING THE RULES

Just when we're sighing in relief and applauding the imagination of the series, they pull another rabbit out of a hat by having Sam leap into the season ending cliffhanger as Sam appears in the body of Lee Harvey Oswald just weeks before the JFK assassination. The biggest surprise in this was that up until then, the series had deliberately steered clear of having Sam Beckett appear in the form of any historical figures. This time, Donald Bellisario had a personal ax to grind.

"Everyone seems to be on the conspiracy bandwagon, but I've never been on it," Bellisario stated in the September 22, 1992 LOS ANGELES TIMES. "But I guess what really struck me the strongest was when my 12-year-old son went to see [Oliver Stone's] 'JFK' and came home totally brainwashed by the film and started telling me all of these half-truths, falsehoods and speculation as if they were fact. I decided if I could figure out a way to bring the tale closer to the truth—no one knows the truth and no one will probably ever know it precisely—but put forth another argument, another theory, another side to the story, that would be a good thing to do."

In this episode, Sam turns up in Oswald at different points in his adult life during the two hour episode. But for the first time, things begin going wrong. Oswald's residual personality begins to gain sway over Sam, especially on the morning of Nov. 22, 1963. In 1999, Al tries talking to Oswald where he's being held, but Oswald won't budge from his position, or even believe what Al is telling him. He smirks a lot. The episode ends with Sam leaping into the body of one of the secret service men riding in the motorcade. While Kennedy is still assassinated, Al reveals that they did change history, because originally Jackie was killed as well.

Adding to the background of this episode is the fact that in 1959, Bellisario actually had an encounter with Oswald which is included in the script. Bellisario had recently gotten out of the Marines and had returned to the base at Tustin to visit some of his Marine buddies. There he encountered another Marine who was reading a radical newspaper. He recalled, "Here's this Marine telling me something that I would expect to hear coming out of Radio Moscow, a whole load of communist doctrine. I got incensed, and if you brought up something he didn't like, he just kind of sneered at you. Finally I just walked away and I asked another Marine there, 'What the hell is with this jerk?' and he said, 'Oh, he does that to everyone. He's harmless.' "

Originally Bellisario had stated that aside from not wanting to deal with major historical events, due to the ripple effect they would have in time were they dramatically altered, he also wished to avoid the obvious, such as tackling something like the Kennedy assassination.

ALWAYS A NEW TWIST

"I was a little surprised about his breaking the rules," Dean Stockwell admitted, "but I sensed why he was doing it. We're going into our fifth season and instead of continuing on with the same old pattern, I think it's the right time to give the audience something different. To add a new color. I think it was a wise idea." Bellisario also admitted to toying with the idea of doing episodes involving Elvis Presley, Richard Nixon or Marilyn Monroe.

The season continued to try different things. A three part episode had Sam leaping through a person's life three times to solve a murder. An evil leaper has been introduced, someone from further in the future than Sam who doesn't have the benevolent ideals exemplified by Beckett.

Even though the going for QUANTUM LEAP has been rocky at times, it has managed to persevere and is presently syndicated on the USA network five nights a week. In some respects the series is a surprise success. Whether it will help to spawn additional science fiction series is doubtful because whenever something unusual is a success, programmers deem it a "non-repeatable phenomenon," which is a fancy way of saying that they don't understand the show and haven't a clue how to imitate it.

In the meantime fans will just keep time tripping with Dr. Samuel Beckett and exploring our recent past from ground level.

Just as rumors begin to emerge that THE NEXT GENERA-

TION will only run through a seventh season, another new television

version of STAR TREK is aimed at the small screen.

January 1993 marks the deep space launch of STAR TREK—DEEP SPACE NINE. Ironically this was announced shortly after the death of Gene Roddenberry. The timing led to speculation that had Roddenberry lived, this series wouldn't have. Suspicions along these lines were raised particularly after descriptions of this new series filtered out. "It's going to be darker and grittier than THE NEXT GENERATION," executive producer Rick Berman stated in the March 6, 1992 ENTERTAINMENT WEEKLY. "The characters won't be squeaky clean."

And yet to the fans, STAR TREK has always meant just that—squeaky clean heroes. What would Gene Roddenberry have thought of this? After all, people close to him have stated that Gene hated STAR TREK VI merely because it postulated Enterprise crew members who were anti-Klingon bigots.

Rick Berman insists that DEEP SPACE NINE is not going to be his and executive producer Michael Piller's own personal take on STAR TREK. He states that this will be just another way of expressing Gene Roddenberry's vision which will be fitting and consistent with everything that has been done with STAR TREK before. In fact, DEEP SPACE NINE was developed under Gene's guidance and with his input.

Regarding Roddenberry's influence on DEEP SPACE NINE, Piller explained, "Every writer knows that we have a responsibility to maintain his vision. We take it very seriously. I got a letter from twenty-five grade school children, and the teacher, who said, 'Please, we use STAR TREK as an example of life in the future and the optimistic view and the hope that Gene gave us. We've heard that this is going to be dark and dreary.' And the truth is that it is not."

CONFLICT IS GOOD

"The truth is that there is more conflict," Pillar said, trying to put the show and its various elements into perspective, "that we're in a part of the universe that is giving us more conflict. And the fact that we are on an alien space station instead of the Enterprise will allow us to do that. But it is the same Gene Roddenberry optimism for the future of mankind that drives the vision of this show. There is not going to be any more shooting, more weapons or battles or anything like that. Certainly we're going to have action. It's going to be an adventure show and it's an entertainment show. We wanted to find the camaraderie that existed in the original STAR TREK, like that relationship between McCoy and Spock, and in order to do that you have to have differ-

ences, and differences between the characters on THE NEXT GENERATION are not so clearly defined."

Michael Piller never had any doubt that there was room for a third STAR TREK series. He feels that Gene Roddenberry created a huge universe of characters and concepts. "Gene used to say, somewhat in kidding, but in a way to communicate what he wanted to do with STAR TREK, that space was like the old west, and that STAR TREK was like WAGON TRAIN. In that whole genre of the west there were dozens of television shows. In the universe that Gene has created there is room, not only for a WAGON TRAIN, but also for a GUNSMOKE. In essence what I think we're doing is the counterpart to the kind of shows you saw on the old west where you have a Ft. Sheridan on the edge of the frontier, and a frontier town in a very active area with a lot of people coming through it."

It started back in October of 1991, when Piller and Berman began developing the show and decided to set the series in the same time frame as THE NEXT GENERATION. "That was a decision made consciously to take advantage of all of the alien races; the universe that has been developed over the last five years of THE NEXT GENERATION. Because we have characters we want to bring onto DEEP SPACE NINE that we've seen on THE NEXT GENERATION and we love. We've got political situations. We've got relationships with the Romulans, Klingons, and Cardassians."

The Cardassians form the continuing threat in the series as the space station is right on the edge of

Cardassian space. The Bajoran home world, which is the planet which Deep Space Nine is in orbit around, was ravaged by the Cardassians before they left it as they were overthrown by the Bajorans in a civil war. This left the Bajorans in a sorry state as the planet had been so severely damaged in the war that the Bajorans were left with nothing to rebuild with. This is why the Bajorans have turned to the Federation and requested admission. The brutality and ruthlessness of the Cardassians is made particularly evident in the episode "Chain Of Command."

POLITICAL ROOTS

The presence of warring cultures was also key to the basis of the series. "Our whole goal was to create more conflict everywhere you turn in this series. So what you have as a result are people who have different agendas. You've got Major Kira, who is a Bajoran, who really doesn't want the Federation to be there, and as a result she and Sisko are in conflict. You've got Odo and Quark who are in conflict. You've got Sisko and Quark who are in conflict. Everywhere you turn you've got conflict in the show. But what we found as a result of that is not only good drama, but a lot more humor than we expected to have.

"The idea for DEEP SPACE NINE grew out of the political situation that we created for a show called 'Ensign Ro' last season on NEXT GENERATION. We did not create Ensign Ro as a potential spin-off, but for all intents and purposes, that's where the tableau was set for this." Berman and Piller wrote several different versions of the series bible while it was being developed. When they finally showed a later version to Paramount, the studio had its own input into the project. In fact, Brandon Tarticoff (before he left Paramount) suggested that the show might be something like THE RIFLEMAN in outer space.

The studio's suggestions were weighed and incorporated into the series concept to produce the final result used now. The father and son element that Brandon was talking about did appeal to Berman and Piller and that element is very much a part of the series. The series bible is called that because it serves as the basis of development for the entire series. All of the characters and their relationships are outlined in it as well as the background of everything used in the series.

Rick Berman and Michael Piller are both veterans of THE NEXT GENERATION and Piller came on board following experiences writing on staff for SIMON AND SIMON and MIAMI VICE. Piller got involved in television first as a journalist. He began in CBS Hollywood checking the accuracy of docudramas. His ambition was to become a producer to protect what he wrote because of all the rewriting which is done to television scripts. Piller had also previously worked on the short-lived science fiction series HARD TIME ON PLANET EARTH. He became acquainted with producer Maurice Hurley who invited him to meet with Gene Roddenberry which led to an episode assignment.

LEARNING THE VISION

Shortly after this Maurice Hurley left THE NEXT GENERA-TION and Piller was invited to join the production staff as Maurice Hurley's successor. "For the next year or so," said Piller, "Gene was really on my case and certainly Rick was on my case, day after day, we went through the creative process as I began to learn to see life through Gene Roddenberry's eyes. Even as he became sick and trusted Rick and I more and more to execute this vision, to this day, even in death, he is an extraordinary influence on both of us."

Michael Piller's job as executive producer of DEEP SPACE NINE primarily involves overseeing the writing and development of ideas for the series. In this capacity he oversees the staff writers and works with the writer of each and every script. Rick Berman participates in that somewhat while Berman also contributes to Berman's specialty, which is overseeing the production, editing, postproduction, music and those aspects of producing the series.

DEEP SPACE NINE is set aboard a space station in orbit around the planet Bajor. The space station is being used by the Cardassians to exploit the mining resources of the Bajoran home world. When the Bajorans finally overthrow the despotic rule of the Cardassians, the Federation places personnel aboard Deep Space Nine to oversee its operation and make sure everything stays cordial and cooperative. When the Federation personnel will not be acting as police, their presence is consciously there to discourage the Cardassians from trying to bother the newly liberated Bajorans. Since the Bajorans have applied for membership in the

143

Federation, their presence there is by the invitation of Bajor.

The Bajorans have been seen previously as they are the race to which Ensign Ro belongs. Ensign Ro was introduced in season four and became a semi-regular on THE NEXT GENERATION in season five. She was most prominently featured in the fifth season in the episode "The Next Phase." While Ensign Ro is an ex-terrorist who was more-or-less drafted into Starfleet due to her expertise in certain matters, DEEP SPACE NINE will deal with a different aspect of the Bajorans. Ensign Ro was initially announced as appearing in this new series, but the actress, Michelle Forbes, chose to bow out to pursue other projects.

RO IS OUT OF THE BIBLE

"We had intended to bring that character with us to DEEP SPACE NINE," Michael Piller explained on the QVC cable channel on Dec. 5, 1992, "but the actress, who we love, Michelle Forbes, simply wasn't interested in doing a series. So after we had actually written a bible and created a script, we had to write that character out of it." A different actor, Nana Visitor, has been cast in the role of the Bajoran regular on the series. She plays Major Kira Nerys, Sisko's first officer and the station's Bajoran attaché. She stated, "The thing that is the most exciting is the script, and the fact that the women in the show are very strong, very powerful, and that it's a lot to do with what's going on in the world right now." Kira Nerys will be portrayed as a strong action hero of the kind who would even lead a rescue mission.

The space station was established by the Cardassians and the Bajorans in conjunction with other alien races. As a result it reflects cultural needs and biases often unfamiliar to some Starfleet personnel. The station was considered of remote interest until the first fixed, stationary wormhole was discovered near the star system where Bajora is located. This wormhole, due to its non-fluctuating nature, can be explored and plotted and is the first stable wormhole known to exist. It's also discovered that it can be used as a gateway to a distant, unexplored quadrant of the galaxy. A new starship class, called the Runabout, makes its first appearance in this series. The wormhole will form a key element of the series, and Piller states that, "Some very strange things have already come out of it in the first ten show."

Set in the year 2360 A.D., the new series is contemporary with THE NEXT GENERATION. While the extent of cross-overs between the two series have yet to be fully determined, STAR TREK—DEEP SPACE NINE will be launched with a two hour premiere which at the very least will include a stopover from the Enterprise and Jean-Luc Picard. Starfleet personnel accustomed to the clean, modern conveniences of starship life will find very different things to contend with aboard the space station. These will reportedly include a casino and a holographic brothel as the space station also serves as a port of call for merchant ships.

The direction of stories hasn't yet been revealed, but the proximity to a wormhole which leads to an unexplored region of the galaxy seems to indicate that expeditions in that direction will form as much of the storyline as explorations into the greasy underside of a rundown space station will.

THE NEW CHARACTERS

DEEP SPACE NINE is slated to feature seven or eight regular characters. The commander of the space station is Benjamin Sisko, a Starfleet captain who was serving with his wife on board one of the vessels attacked by Picard when he had been transformed into Locutus of Borg. The man's wife was killed in the attack and he had been rotated back to Earth in semi-retirement to recover from the ordeal. His command of the space station is his first active duty post since his wife was killed about three years before. Needless to say, he harbors some ill will towards Picard and finds it difficult to accept that Picard was *completely* helpless to stop the attack. Along with him on Deep Space Nine is Sisko's son, Jake, played by Cirroc Lofton.

"We felt that a father and son relationship would be a different relationship than any other STAR TREK kind of hero that we've seen before," Piller explained. When Sisko first arrives at the space station, he doesn't consider it a very good assignment. The station is not operating very well and it seems to be an assignment on the edge of nowhere.

As Piller described the character, "He has found himself at a place in his life that he can't quite get beyond and he's sent to this space station. He doesn't like this assignment because the space station was built by the Cardassians who have just abandoned it. The Bajorans are struggling with the potential of civil war. It's in the middle of nowhere, when we start the show, and he's given this job and basically Picard is there to greet him when he gets to Deep Space Nine."

Sisko is not happy with his assignment, but all this changes when the stable wormhole is discovered and the importance of station Deep Space Nine becomes elevated immeasurably in the eyes of the Federation. In further describing this character, Piller said, "He is

DEEPSPACE NINE continues the tradition of STAR TREK, set in the same time as THE NEXT GENERATION.

sent on a quest and in this whole pilot episode it is a personal quest for this man who has lost his way and must conquer the dragon (in another genre). In this, case he must conquer his personal dragons in order to move on with his life and to grow as a man and to be a good father and to be a good officer. What we will find in this show is a man who is coming to Deep Space Nine, but is coming to find himself."

SHIFTY CHARACTERS

Another character is a shape-shifter, Odo, who is also a security officer. This alien came from a world on the other side of the wormhole, but he does not remember his past, having been found as an infant aboard a drifting spacecraft. In order to fit in among the people who found him, he has chosen to adopt a humanoid form,

145

but his efforts at maintaining this form are imperfect. The producers have stated that this character will be used to explore the nature of humanity and what truly defines one as being human. In this way he will occupy the position of Spock and Data as those characters have been used to act as a mirror of humanity in the other two STAR TREK series.

Being neither part human nor an android, the take will be completely different from that taken with either Spock or Data. Odo is being played by Rene Auberjonois and is already being touted as one of the main characters to emerge from the series. "He is the curmudgeon of all curmudgeons," Piller stated. "So instead of Data who worships humanity and wants to be that, and Spock who would deny it, Odo looks at him and because he has been forced to pass as a humanoid all of his life, to look like us and act like us because it's a lot more socially acceptable than being a chair all your life if you're a shape-shifting lifeform, he sort of resents it. So he has now found a way to use it as a defense mechanism and keep a distance from it and find ways to be critical of the human condition."

The alien's actual appearance is a formless blob. "He is only one of a kind," Piller revealed. "He was found near where this wormhole shows up, as an infant in a spacecraft, which we are going to assume probably came out of the Gamma Quadrant. He has no idea where he came from and he's always searching for his identity."

Regarding the makeup which disguises the actor somewhat, he explained, "It's a mask but it feeds what I feel is in the script for the character and I find it very evocative." One plot thread which has been revealed regarding Odo is that Majel Barrett will appear at some point as Lwaxana Troi and will become a romantic interest for the alien shapeshifter. When he reveals to her that he has to turn into a bucket of liquid every night, she unhesitatingly replies, "That's okay. I can swim."

A NEW ALLY

The alien, Odo, had come out of the wormhole in a spacecraft fifty years before and had served the Cardassians on the space station long before Starfleet determined that Deep Space Nine had strategic importance. Odo adopted human form in an effort to better acclimate to this galaxy and the people he encounters. The alien is just as willing to assist Starfleet as he has aided the Cardassians for the past half century. With Starfleet planning to explore the galaxy through the wormhole, he believes that he may at last uncover the clues he needs to unlock the secrets to his past.

Colm Meany, whose role as Miles O'Brien, the Transporter Chief, has been growing on THE NEXT GENERATION, is transferred from the Enterprise in the premiere episode of DEEP SPACE NINE where he will become Master of Operations on the new series. His character changes are explored as the viewers compare his Enterprise duties with his duties on Deep Space NINE.

"We've always thought he was a terrific performer," Piller stated, "and now we're giving him something much more interesting

146

to do as a leading character on the new show. He is pulling his hair out from one minute to the next because everything is breaking down. He can't get the replicators to make a good cup of coffee; his wife Keiko is terribly unhappy about having been taken off the Enterprise and come over to this dreadful space station. So he finds himself in an uncomfortable position."

The science officer aboard the space station is played by Terry Farrell, who appeared in HELL-RAISER III. Farrell plays Lt. Jadzia Dax, an alien known as a Trill. The Trill were introduced in the NEXT GENERATION episode "The Host," where we were shown that the Trill are a dual species that join to become a single entity. Since the sex of the host body is unimportant to the Trill, the three hundred year old Dax now inhabits the body of a young woman. Previously Dax inhabited the body of an older man who was a mentor of Captain Benjamin Sisko's. But in its new body, Sisko finds that he's physically attracted to Dax.

Originally they had conceived Dax as being a very serene and focused character, but according to Piller, "The more we've written her, the more we're finding that she is not what she appears to be. That underneath this placid exterior, there's all these various personalities that she's gone through that are in turmoil and there's a lot of inner conflict. You know all the voices we hear inside of ourselves are all made up of different subpersonalities; well she's got them all screaming at her in a variety of different ways."

ALWAYS A PLAN

On the human side again, Siddig El Fadil plays Dr. Julian Bashir, a Starfleet medical officer in his mid-twenties. His youth and inexperience will be emphasized since he has just graduated from Starfleet Medical and this is his first post outside of the Sol system. Bashir thinks he knows it all and has a knack for rubbing people the wrong way.

Armin Shimerman plays a Ferengi bartender named Quark in the new series—one of the shifty, untrustworthy aliens introduced in year one of THE NEXT GENERATION. He has his hands into all sorts of illegal and improper activities going on behind the scenes aboard Deep Space Nine. His ongoing presence will be one of the constant conflicts aboard Deep Space Nine, but as a series regular, he'll be in a position to have a more fully developed character than any Ferengi presented to date. In fact, he will forge a friendship of sorts with Benjamin Sisko, and will be liked (but not entirely trusted) by his compatriots.

The actor explains that, like THE NEXT GENERATION, in DEEP SPACE NINE the staff has created, "fascinating aliens that have three sides." One of the more interesting relationships on the show is that between Quark and Odo, the shape-shifting security officer as they're sworn enemies who have an on-going verbal conflict. Even before the series aired those involved with the show were predicting that Quark would emerge as the most popular character.

Executive producer and series co-creator Michael Pillar has

147

stated that it wouldn't be out of the question to see such characters as Q or Lwaxana Troi turn up on the series. This could also mean appearances by Klingons, Romulans and perhaps even the Borg. While the producers have revealed that the Enterprise and Captain Picard are definitely slated to appear in the premiere episode, how full the crew roster of the Enterprise will be in that story is still being negotiated.

The reason that Paramount wanted a new STAR TREK television series to run concurrent with THE NEXT GENERATION is that Paramount presently envisions ST—TNG lasting seven seasons, which will give the studio a healthy syndication package of about 170 episodes. DEEP SPACE NINE will run concurrent with the last year and a half of the first run episodes of NEXT GENERATION. This will serve to help establish DEEP SPACE NINE so that when THE NEXT GENERATION goes into reruns, a new and different STAR TREK series will already have been established and be in place in the syndication market. STAR TREK—DEEP SPACE NINE is being syndicated with another new Paramount series, a revival of the fifties series THE UNTOUCH-ABLES.

By establishing DEEP SPACE NINE as being contempo-rary with THE NEXT GENERA-TION, even after TNG goes off the air, characters from that series could still turn up on the new series. With the highly rated appearance of James Doohan on THE NEXT GENERATION in the fall of 1992, Doohan has been urg-ing Paramount to add him to the cast of DEEP SPACE NINE. Less certain are rumors about Shatner expressing interest in participating in DEEP SPACE NINE.

It's hard to believe that back in the seventies, many people were saying that STAR TREK was just old news and that nothing would ever be done with the premise again.

Science fiction on television fills a very narrow spectrum, never better exemplified than by SPACE: 1999 and BAT-TLESTAR: GALACTICA. The shows are what producers often believe science fiction to be.

The early Seventies was a pretty bleak period for science fiction on television. With the exception of the occasional TV movie done by Gene Roddenberry in an effort to prove that he had a creative life after STAR TREK, not a lot was happening. It wasn't until STAR WARS was released in 1977 that television producers practically tripped over each other trying to duplicate that success on television—and none of them ever did.

The reason none of them ever succeeded was readily presented in SPACE: 1999. While the only thing television producers tend to learn from other people's mistakes is how to repeat them, they almost never learn from anyone's success, except how to imitate the most superficial elements. When BATTLESTAR: GALACTICA came along a few years later, this was all too readily demonstrated. They just didn't get it.

Prior to SPACE: 1999, producers Gerry & Sylvia Anderson (a husband and wife team) had made a successful career of producing children's action adventure shows in which the characters were all played by marionettes and extensive use was made of special effects miniatures. These shows included SUPERCAR, THUNDERBIRDS, CAPTAIN SCARLET, STINGRAY and FIREBALL XL5. All of these were produced in the Sixties on small budgets but were modest successes. THUNDERBIRDS was successful enough to spawn two motion pictures, although none of the other series matched the THUNDERBIRDS in popularity.

But the Andersons grew increasingly tired of producing puppet shows for children and wanted to graduate into live action. They did this first with the syndicated series UFO, a show about a secret British government project to track and combat flying saucers which are landing on Earth and kidnapping human beings for nefarious purposes. Although uneven, the series had its moments and its 26 episode first season seemed destined to move into a second. But instead, the producers decided to develop a new series called SPACE JOURNEY 1999. Previous titles considered for the series include JOURNEY INTO SPACE, SPACE INTRUDERS and SPACE PROBE. As of 1973 it still had the form of a spin-off from UFO, using the moonbase common to both shows as the starting point.

THE START

Originally "Moon City" existed as part of an early warning system against alien attack, just as the moon base did in UFO. Moon City, according to an early premise, was 20 miles square and included for defense two different types of vehicles. One was

SF FAILURES
SPACE 1999
& BATTLESTAR

the Interceptor (as seen on UFO), and the others were Lunarmobiles which were equipped with ground-to-ground missiles to deal with ufo's which landed on the surface of the Moon. On the non-defense side was a Moonship shuttle (for forerunner of the Eagle spacecraft ultimately used on SPACE: 1999). There were even Moonbuggies for exploring the surface.

Whereas UFO had starred all British actors, the Andersons decided to go for a gold and produce a series which they could sell directly to American network television. The Sixties British series THE AVENGERS had managed to graduate to success in American prime time, along with THE PRISONER, and the Andersons hoped to use that interest in British adventure television to gain themselves admittance to American prime time.

They cast the show with actors familiar to American audiences. Initially the parts of John Koenig and Helena Russell were conceived for Robert Culp and Katherine Ross, who were both fairly well known from film and television in the early Seventies. But ultimately Martin Landau and Barbara Bain (who had appeared on the first two years of MISSION: IMPOSSIBLE) were cast as the leads. Barry Morse, well known from his recurring role on the highly popular Sixties series THE FUGITIVE, played Professor Victor Bergman.

In a supporting role as Alan Carter, Moonbase Alpha's chief Eagle pilot, was Nick Tate. An Australian actor, Tate had appeared in many TV shows down under before deciding to relocate to

England in the early Seventies. Initially he was cast as Alan Carter's co-pilot and was signed for only the pilot, but then was asked to do five more. The character worked out so well that Tate was signed for the rest of the season, and was retained for year two as well.

During the time that season two was in production, Tate was asked his opinion of the first season, and the actor stated, "I think I agree with the general public that there wasn't enough emotion and humor in the first season. This year that's been rectified. I always wanted to see development of the secondary characters, which has happened. I think we were all very much aware of the series' faults, but we weren't aware of them when the show started. It was something that became apparent as the series wore on. But then, there wasn't very much we could do about it because the format and style were set. The only way we could do anything was to start a second season."

FULL SPEED AHEAD

The Andersons wanted to go all out on SPACE 1999 and ATV (Associated Television) under Sir Lew Grade, approved a suitable budget, which according to some reports may have been as high as $300,000 per episode. Subsequent information revealed that the budgets were considerably less. When you're trying to sell a major series to a network, you don't brag about how cheap it is. But in spite of the producers' track record, the three major networks at that time (ABC, NBC & CBS) turned the show down. In that time before the advent of cable television, the only alternative left was syndication. Abe Mandell, the president of ITC (a subsidiary of ATC) sold the show directly to American television stations, city by city, until they managed to sell to 155 stations. Out of that number, 88 of them actually pre-empted regular network programming with the series.

The series premiered in September 1975 to initial enthusiasm which was quickly met with disappointment. Unlike UFO, which had occasional scenes in outer space involving a Moonbase, SPACE: 1999 (shortened from the earlier much longer title) was set entirely in outer space with the Moon being the base of operations.

The first episode, "Breakaway," opens in September 1999 when John Koenig is named the new commander of Moonbase Alpha, just as a signals are picked up from a previously unknown planet named Meta. There is pressure on to launch a deep space probe shortly after Koenig's arrival. But Koenig argues against this until he can determine the source of mysterious ailments striking various members of the moonbase colony which he believes deserve more immediate attention. The moonbase is part of a project to oversee a dumping ground for nuclear waste on the dark side of the moon. Many nations from Earth contribute nuclear waste to the dump and so there is political pressure to insure that this extraterrestrial disposal area for hazardous waste remain viable as no nation on Earth will tolerate the radioactive waste being stored in their borders.

Moonbase Alpha is meant to be self-sustaining as it engages in various research projects, includ-

ing keeping a watchful eye on the nuclear dump. The problems are soon traced to the dump, which creates political problems because Earth needs that dump to dispose of its nuclear waste. Koenig is pressured to launch the probe by his superior, Commissioner Simmonds, in spite of reports on problems at the dump. But while they're arguing over what to do, a chain reaction occurs in the dump causing a massive discharge of magnetic radiation. The explosion is of such magnitude that the Moon is hurled out of orbit into space. The vehicles they have on Moonbase, called Eagles, are built for short runs only and at any rate would not be able to evacuate all of the Moonbase Alpha personnel back to Earth. The last transmission that Moonbase Alpha receives from Earth indicates that the Earth has been rocked by disasters and cannot render any aid.

PHYSICS 101

The premise was shaky from the start since an explosion so powerful that it would have actually ripped the moon out of orbit would have shattered the moon and done only slightly less damage to the Earth as the moon's own gravity affects earth as well. Had the moon broken up and Moonbase Alpha been hurled away on a fragment, that would have been much more believable. But even a thin, unbelievable premise can be accepted if the series produces stories worth telling and which are well told. Sadly, SPACE: 1999 could never have been accused of that.

The problem with SPACE: 1999, and with many other television shows born in the Seventies, is that it was decided by someone, somewhere that a storyline should be simple enough so that even if someone tunes in halfway through there'll be no trouble following what's going on. The other side of this is that people who tuned in at the beginning of the episode will become bored by the lack of story movement. Even within those narrow confines the stories were overly simplistic, and as Isaac Asimov put it at the time, the show was "scientifically preposterous." In an article he wrote for the NEW YORK TIMES, Asimov maintained that the errors were made not for dramatic effect, which could be forgiven, but out of sheer ignorance.

An example of the storytelling deficiencies is the episode "Force Of Life." We never find out what the "Force Of Life" of the title is or what its purpose is in invading Moonbase Alpha and wrecking havoc as it steals energy before moving off back into space at the end of the episode. Oddly enough, back in the mid-Seventies Martin Landau appeared on a talk show while SPACE: 1999 was still in its original run, and another guest on the talk show, actor Buster Crabbe (who played Flash Gordon and Buck Rogers in the 1930's), asked Landau about this particular episode of SPACE: 1999. Crabbe wanted to know what it been all about and why the alien entity was there and what it had wanted. Landau had no idea what the story had meant, and readily admitted it.

SPACE: 1999 met with its harshest criticism from two fronts—hard core science fiction fans and STAR TREK fans. The hard core SF fans recognized the scientific implausibilities and became incensed over the continuous violations of science and physics in the first episode alone. STAR TREK fans turned away from the show because they'd been spoiled by STAR TREK. After seeing each episode over and over again, they were certain that any new science fiction series with an outer space setting would have to follow some of the precepts established so well by STAR TREK. But SPACE:1999 ignored them. STAR TREK's strengths lay in its scripts and in its well defined characters, of which SPACE: 1999 offered neither. In 1975 the chances of STAR TREK ever being revived seemed remote at best. So fans were looking for the "next" STAR TREK. They were willing to give *any* new SF series a chance. All it had to do was meet them halfway.

CRASH LANDING

By the end of the first year, SPACE: 1999 was in ratings trouble. So what did they do? They hired one of the producers who worked on STAR TREK. This was also done because Gerry and Sylvia Anderson's marriage was breaking up and so she stepped down from her role as producer.

Fred Freiberger, who replaced Gene Roddenberry as the line producer on the third year of STAR TREK in 1968-69, was hired to revamp the show and try to make it more appealing to American audiences. The fact that Freiberger was universally regarded as making STAR TREK *less appealing* in its final season was a fact that Gerry Anderson was apparently unaware of. But Freiberger had other credits, including producing or otherwise contributing to such series as THE WILD WILD WEST, PETROCELLI and STARSKY AND HUTCH.

The revamping of the third year included an emphasis on action/adventure storylines and the addition of Catherine Schell to the cast as Maya, a shape-shifting alien. In order to address some of the criticism the series had received, the second season premiere, "Metamorph," included a Moonbase Alpha log entry which explained that shortly after the Moon had been hurled out of Earth's orbit, it entered a time warp which spit the Moon out light years away in uncharted space. Thus the mysterious alien worlds they kept encountering were explained.

The budget for the first year of SPACE: 1999 was reported as being $6,500,000. Although ITC sent out a publicity release reporting that the overall budget for the second season swelled to $7,200,000 (or $300,000 per episode), Fred Freiberger dismissed that as being just a lot of hype. The producer maintained that the true per episode budget was $185,000 which still enabled the company to obtain superior production values. This had to do with the fact that at the time the British pound was worth $1.80 American, plus below the line production costs are much less in England. A scene in which Maya leaps into the are and transforms into a black panther in mid-leap took all day to film and cost $5,000 compared to a cost of $50,000 to spend an entire day shooting in the United States on a major studio production.

FRED TELLS IT LIKE IT IS

In the November 1980 issue of STARLOG, Fred Freiberger was interviewed and related what he viewed as the problems of SPACE: 1999 when he was hired to revamp it.

"They were doing the show as an English show where there was no story, with the people standing around and talking. They had good concepts, they have wonderful characters, but they kept talking about the same thing and there was no plot development. 1999 opened extremely well in the United States and then went right down the tubes. There was nobody you cared about in the show. Nobody at all. The people themselves didn't care about each other. I did a whole thing where I at least had a scene where somebody said, 'My God! He's gonna be hurt! Is he dead? Is he alive?' They just didn't do that."

Freiberger felt that the British producers regarded action as meaning that they had to blow up another Eagle, which he curtailed in the second season. After the second series wound to a close, ITC still held out hope for bringing it back as a possible mid-season re-entry, assuming they could get enough American television stations to sign up for more episodes. Had they been able to accomplish this, they would have quickly reunited the cast and filmed as additional thirteen episodes. But this never happened. SPACE: 1999 ended its two year run with a total package of 48 episodes.

While the second season was certainly different from the first, the writing was only marginally better. Characterization at least existed, but the stories were on the

155

level of Saturday morning kids shows and not the kind of science fiction stories people had found they could respect on OUTER LIMITS, TWILIGHT ZONE and THE OUTER LIMITS.

TIME WILL TELL

The mark of a good series is how well it stands up to the test of time. For a few years after the show's cancellation, an annual SPACE: 1999 convention was held in the United States. While at first attendance was strong, interest began to peter out. While the initial SPACE: 1999 conventions drew a couple thousand people, attendance at "Space Con 10" in Los Angeles in July 1992 was estimated to be about three hundred. Fans of SPACE: 1999 can contact Space Con at PO Box 2948, Beverly Hills, CA 90213.

In 1979 when STAR TREK—THE MOTION PICTURE debuted, some of us had a running joke regarding it being SPACE: 1999—THE MOTION PICTURE, because of how dull ST—TMP was and in too many ways it reminded one of SPACE: 1999. But today, with virtually any television series which had any sort of following being plundered for motion picture treatment (including CAR 54, GILLIGAN'S ISLAND, THE BEVERLY HILLBILLIES and THE BRADY BUNCH), I wouldn't be at all surprised if eventually they got around to SPACE: 1999.

BATTLESTAR GALACTICA

Back in 1978 the rumors and articles about the forthcoming ABC-TV series BATTLESTAR GALACTICA had been running wild in the press for months. It was to be the most expensive series ever made for television. Hopes were flying high. For the first time ever, TV was doing a science fiction series where the budget ballooned to meet the demands of the story rather than the story contracting to meet the demands of the budget. The sky was the limit. So how come the horizon turned out to be so bleak?

The three hours premiere on Sept. 17, 1978 was promising and often even effective. Using a Pearl Harbor premise in which a peace negotiation was just a mask for a wholesale attack, things were exciting and interesting, up to a point. Some fine moments were had when the Galactica returned to the home planet of Caprica only to find it in ruins.

Thereafter it has the "ragtag fleet" assembling. There's even a prolonged sequence consisting of clearing space mines. The mine-clearing sequence pointed up a problem with the series which was often repeated. The producers of the show didn't understand that in outer space, certain principles can be applied which wouldn't work on an earthbound show. For instance, you can detour around obstacles because of how vast space is. Fuel is expended only for maneuvering, getting up to speed and slowing down. Inertia and the lack of friction handles the rest. Unlike in cars, boats and airplanes, fuel isn't being burnt the entire time the craft is moving. And yet the Galactica is constantly shown with its massive engines burning and firing as though it would stop if it wasn't doing this. They just didn't get it. An entire two-part episode ("The

Gun On Ice Planet Zero") is reduced to pointlessness over such details.

The characters introduced in this opening episode are a mixed bag of successful and unsuccessful ideas. Richard Hatch as Captain Apollo is a sensitive, believable character. His relationships with people work because we believe that he cares about what he is doing. On the other hand, Dirk Benedict as Starbuck is as cliché as they come. His character has no dimension whatsoever and is just a macho womanizer who is apparently there to off balance Apollo lest the audience think that the show's only heroic figure is a wimp because he shows his feelings.

GET REAL

Starbuck is always pursuing this woman or that and usually more than one at a time. Starbuck came across as nothing more than a moronic pilot (a contradiction in terms since a pilot would need to be quite intelligent to operate the technical hardware displayed on the series). The only time that this character was handled in a sensitive and therefore atypical manner was in the revival of the series when it was transmogrified into GALACTICA: 1980.

In the episode "The Return of Starbuck," we learn that Starbuck was marooned on a planet where he repaired and befriended a Cylon warrior robot. This is by no means a new idea as the concept of two enemies becoming friends when marooned together was previously used as the plot of an episode of the old UFO series as well as the movie ENEMY MINE. And both of those got the idea from the 1968

film HELL IN THE PACIFIC which starred Lee Marvin and Toshiro Mifune in a second World War setting. But nonetheless, "The Return of Starbuck" handled the concept with grace and sensitivity as even the Cylon robot became a character instead of a fighting machine. That was certainly a twist as up until then every Cylon was portrayed as being identical with every other Cylon.

The Cylons were basically an army of Darth Vaders who were nothing more than droning machines. They were originally conceived as something more. The Cylons were supposed to be an alien race whose brains were housed in robot bodies. But this idea was nixed by the networks because they feared that if the Cylons were living in any manner then it would be deemed a "violent" show because so many beings were being slaughtered each week. But blowing the crap out of robots, well, in the words of Emily Letella, "That's very different." But this origin of the Cylons is preserved and explored in the novelization of the pilot done by author Robert Thurston (based on Glen Larson's script). Examining this origin concept, though, one is also reminded of the Daleks, a robot race in the British TV series DR. WHO.

The father figure of GALACTICA is Lorne Greene. Unfortunately, Greene had a high recognizability factor from his decade plus on BONANZA and so it wasn't long before the show was known far and wide among its detractors as BATTLESTAR PONDEROSA. Greene was an effective enough actor, but he tended to have only two expressions—stern and happy with nothing in-between.

A WOMAN WITH TASTE

Jane Seymour as Serina was the most interesting female character on the show. She only lasted three episodes and right after leaving GALACTICA she became a major television star. Many people don't remember that she was in motion pictures as far back as the first Roger Moore James Bond film LIVE AND LET DIE. Her TV work has garnered her a lot of attention while movie stardom has continued to elude her in spite of such fine roles as in the film SOMEWHERE IN TIME with Christopher Reeve.

Serina was the mother of Boxey (Noah Hathaway), which introduced an odd subplot. Back on Caprica, Boxey's little dog was killed in the attack and the little boy became virtually catatonic over the loss of his pet daggit. Thus a robot daggit was created for him aboard the Galactica (in reality this was a chimp in a costume, which was certainly a first since the costume was completely self-contained and most animals would suffer from claustrophobia in such conditions). All is well with Boxey after that and Apollo even marries his mother. But in the third episode, "Lost Planet of Gods," Boxey's mother, Serina, is killed. The episode ends with Apollo and Boxey going off to console each other. Amazingly the boy takes his mother's death much better than he did the death of his dog!

Because GALACTICA was bought as a series and rushed into production, the scripts started suffering quickly. But even before that

happened, the show began using stock footage of its own special effects during the premiere episode. While the shot of the Cylon fighter swooping in low over the Galactica is impressive, it becomes less impressive when seen in virtually every show (and at least twice in the pilot alone).

While every special effects shot in STAR WARS was done new without reusing previously printed shots, on television that just can't be matched. As it was the effects people at Apogee found producer Glen Larson to be a harsh task master and a difficult man to work for. They arrived at this conclusion even before the pilot episode was completed.

LOOK CLOSELY

As their way of reply to the difficulties they'd endured under Larson, the technicians arranged the fibreoptics of the lights used on Caprica to spell out a rather well known epithet which employed the most famous of four-letter words in conjunction with the adverb "off." You can only see the two word remark if you're watching for it and know exactly where to look. It's easier to spot it first in the BAT-TLESTAR GALACTICA photonovel about a quarter of the way into the book on the page whose heading reads: "Adama orders the Galactica to leave fleet formation and speed home in an attempt to protect the colonies—but the Cylon attack is already raging. . . ."

The photo at the top of the page shows Cylon ships swooping down high above the city whose lights can be glimpsed far below. There is a Cylon ship in the center of the picture and immediately to its right is the short command spelled out in lights (about a half-an-inch tall in the photonovel) amid many other lights. Once you spot it, it seems to leap out at you when glimpsed on television. On TV it's difficult to notice only because the scene in question is flashed on the screen for less than five seconds. With a videotape (and a good machine which can freeze-frame without causing the image to break up) you can spot it easily. It's an elaborate inside joke but one which Apogee doubtless enjoyed pulling off. My information on this came by way of people who were working at Apogee effects at the time those special effects were shot.

As BATTLESTAR GALACTICA entered its second month of broadcast, it had already fallen into a pit of clichés, and like vipers they were feasting on the series and draining its energy. By November of 1978, the show had become an excruciating blend of bad science fiction and ridiculous plots peopled by cardboard characters.

Then something happened. They ran a two-part episode which actually wasn't half-bad. "The Living Legend" (Nov. 26 & Dec. 3, 1978) is a story featuring Lloyd Bridges as the commander of the Battlestar Pegasus, a ship which had been presumed lost in the final war with the Cylons when the colonies were destroyed. Bridges, as Commander Cain, is not only legendary but a bit on the reckless side. His pilots are blindly loyal to him, even when he suggests an attack on a Cylon base, a maneuver which Adama deems to be suicidal. There results a lot of jockeying for

position and some questioning of Adama's judgment as Cain's reputation blinds people to his battle-worn outlook.

LIKE MOTHER
LIKE DAUGHTER

Also featured in these episodes is Ann Lockhart as Cain's daughter, a character who remained with the series beyond this two-part story. Ann Lockhart, of course, is the daughter of June Lockhart, who starred in the LOST IN SPACE series in the previous decade. Ann Lockhart proved to be a pleasant and engaging young actress who unfortunately hasn't received much additional exposure since the series concluded.

While not a terrific story by any means, "The Living Legend" was much closer to what had been hoped for by the level of expertise displayed in the series' pilot. If each episode of GALACTICA had only been as good as these two, science fiction fans throughout the country wouldn't have started turning the series off in droves by this time. But a lot of bad had already been flushed down the tube, and more was to come, so "The Living Legend" seemed like a fluke—it was a little better planned than most of the other episodes and still holds up well in reruns. The casting of Lloyd Bridges, a presence greatly missed on modern TV, didn't hurt either.

The problem with a lot of these episodes is that only rarely are the characters explored sufficiently enough for us to care about them. Usually they're just character types going through the motions which the script demands of them. The story fills up time without

159

drawing us into the action on an emotionally or psychologically participatory level. It was like SPACE: 1999 all over again.

While the series was canceled in 1979, it was revived a year later, but the less said about GALACTICA 1980 the better. It was basically just BATTLESTAR GALACTICA with the budget slashed and scripts which were, if anything, worse (with the sole exception of "The Return of Starbuck").

DISAPPOINTED

All elements of BAT-TLESTAR GALACTICA which fans of that show liked were eliminated in GALACTICA 1980. It was turned into an earthbound science fiction series in which the lack of its visible budget was matched only by the paucity of imagination of its scripts. When Universal was given a second chance on this series, instead of trying to make a show which was better than BAT-TLESTAR GALACTICA, they delivered it into Glen Larson's hands and he turned it into a series which was worse.

The story editors on GALACTICA 1980 were Chris Bunch and Allan Cole. They were under orders not to rewrite any of Glen Larson's scripts when he turned them in, and the results were presented for all to see. GALACTI-CA 1980 killed science fiction on network television for years, and only the success of STAR TREK—THE NEXT GENERATION in syndication has enticed any of the major networks into trying again, with the sadly derivative SPACE RANGERS.

Why do producers return to this kind of science fiction over and over again with predictable regularity? Because *they* can understand it. It's not "too weird." They are basically just cop shows or westerns with an outer space setting. The problem is that they're written with little regard for this new setting, as though the far future or another planet is no different than downtown Detroit. A prime example is the premiere episode of the 1993 series SPACE RANGERS in which a shape-shifting alien is alien with a bullet. The fact that a bullet would *pass through* a shape-shifter was apparently not understood by the filmmakers.

One aspect of THE NEXT GENERATION which the actors found difficult to adjust to at first was the frequent use of science fiction jargon. Shows like SPACE: 1999, BATTLESTAR GALACTICA and SPACE RANGERS make no attempt to explore futuristic technology and its impacts on humanity, which at its core is what science fiction is essentially about. Technology affects how people live their lives and shapes our culture. Compare the culture of 1893 to 1993 and you'll see that it has been transformed by technology. By ignoring that simple truth, many science fiction television shows never actually seem to be set in the future at all.